ACCORDING
TO
SEASON

BOOKS BY MRS. WILLIAM STARR DANA
(Frances Theodora Parsons)

How to Know the Wild Flowers
According to Season
How to Know the Ferns
Plants and Their Children
Perchance Some Day

EARLY BLUE VIOLET
Viola palmata

ACCORDING TO SEASON

Mrs. William Starr Dana

WITH 16 ORIGINAL COLOR PLATES BY
Elsie Louise Shaw

Houghton Mifflin Company

BOSTON

1990

For information about permission to reproduce selections
from this book, write to Permissions, Houghton Mifflin
Company, 2 Park Street, Boston, Massachusetts 02108.

Library of Congress Cataloging-in-Publication Data

Parsons, Frances Theodora, 1861–1952.
According to season / by Mrs. William Starr Dana.
p.   cm.
Reprint. Originally published: New York : C. Scribner's Sons,
1924.
ISBN 0-395-55413-6
1. Wild flowers — Northeastern States.   2. Seasons — Northeastern
States.   3. Natural history — Northeastern States.   I. Title.
QK118.P2   1990
508.74 — dc20   90-39444
CIP

Printed in the United States of America

BP 10 9 8 7 6 5 4 3 2 1

According to Season was first published in 1894 by Charles Scribner's Sons. This
book is a reprint of the enlarged and illustrated 1902 edition.

CONTENTS

LIST OF
ILLUSTRATIONS

EDITOR'S NOTE

FRANCES THEODORA Smith Dana Parsons was born in 1861 and brought up in New York City. As a child, she spent her summers at her grandparents' place near Newburgh, New York, between the Hudson River and the Catskill Mountains, where she developed what would become a lifelong love of nature in general and wildflowers in particular. This love would have remained undocumented and unexpressed — and American nature writing would have been much the poorer — if not for a personal tragedy and the draconian rules that governed mourning in the Victorian era.

In her early twenties Frances Smith married Commodore William Starr Dana, a naval officer many years older than herself. Within a short period of time she lost her first baby and her husband, who died in a flu epidemic in Paris. Mrs. Dana returned to New York and her family. As a proper Victorian widow, she had to wear black, of course. For the first six months her face would have been hidden behind a smothering ankle-length veil that hung from a regulation bonnet; after six months, she could turn the veil back from her face to rest heavily on her head and shoulders. After a year, narrow white ruching at the neck and wrists was permitted. As Buckner Hollingsworth explained in a biographical sketch of Mrs. Dana, "Little by little, slowly — so slowly — the horror was mitigated until at the end of five years she was once more able to go back into colors."

The conventions of what a widow might do and whom she might see were equally rigid. In the beginning, she associated only with her family and a few close friends. Although gradually she could see more people, it was years before she could go to a party, and she certainly couldn't go dancing while in mourning. As Hollingsworth put it, "Once time had begun to lessen young Mrs. Dana's grief, the years that stretched ahead must have seemed a black crepe-hung purgatory."

She was rescued from this stultifying life by a friend, Marion Satterlee, who lured her into taking walks and resuming her childhood interest in wildflowers. Together the two women roamed the countryside, observing, making notes, and collecting material for a book that became an American classic: *How to Know the Wild Flowers.*

This book, written by Mrs. Dana and illustrated by Marion Satterlee, was an immediate success. The first printing sold out in five days, and *How to Know the Wild Flowers* was reprinted again and again, the cloth edition remaining in print for fifty years. In 1989 a gift edition with new color paintings was published by Houghton Mifflin. Although *How to Know the Wild Flowers* has been supplanted as an identification guide by more recent and more scientific works, no book can compare with Mrs. Dana's for its astute observations, rich and colorful lore, and entertaining writing.

Following publication of *How to Know the Wild Flowers,* Mrs. Dana wrote a column about nature for the *New York Tribune.* In 1894 these essays were published as *According to Season.* An enlarged edition with color plates by Elsie Louise Shaw was published in 1902. Although this book did not have the great success and long life of *How to Know the Wild Flowers,* it is in some ways even more readable than Mrs. Dana's first book. In addition to making marvelous observations about the natural world around her, the author painted an intimate and lively picture of the life and times of a nineteenth-century city dweller. Like the flowers and birds she loved, Mrs. Dana preferred the country but could even celebrate nature on the city streets, where "once or twice I have noticed a flock of juncoes in the city back-yard, driven to town, I suppose, for supplies." At winter's end, she wrote: "Spring is in the cock's crow and the dog's bark. It is in the fresh, stimulating odor that comes up from the earth, just bared to the sunshine. It is no longer wise for the nature-lover to procrastinate."

During the early years of her second marriage, to James Russell Parsons, Jr., Frances Theodora Parsons, as she then signed herself, wrote a guide called *How to Know the Ferns* and a child's botany book. After publishing four books in six years, the last in 1899, she gave up writing to become active in Republican state politics and the suffrage movement. Her privately printed autobiography, *Perchance Some Day,* was published in 1951, a year before her death.

This new edition of *According to Season* is based on the enlarged, illustrated 1902 edition published by Charles Scribner's Sons. Of the original thirty-one color plates, sixteen have been reprinted. The original binding was one of the lesser compositions of Margaret Armstrong, a leading turn-of-the-century designer; we have substituted a different Armstrong design, one of her most beautiful. This binding originally appeared on an 1899 Houghton Mifflin edition of *The Tent on the Beach,* by John Greenleaf Whittier.

FRANCES TENENBAUM
Boston 1990

ACCORDING
TO
SEASON

INTRODUCTORY

Self-sown my stately garden grows;
The winds and wind-blown seed,
Cold April rain and colder snows
My hedges plant and feed.

From mountains far and valleys near
The harvests sown to-day
Thrive in all weathers without fear, —
Wild planters, plant away!

— EMERSON

Behold there in the woods the fine madman . . .
he accosts the grass and the trees; he feels the
blood of the violet, the clover, and the lily in
his veins; and he talks with the brook that wets
his foot.

— EMERSON

THAT WE KNOW so little, as a people, of our birds, trees, rocks, and flowers, is not due, I think, so much to any inborn lack of appreciation of the beautiful or interesting, as to the fact that we have been obliged to concentrate our energies in those directions which seemed to lead to some immediate material advantage, leaving us little time to expend upon the study of such objects as promised to yield no tangible remuneration. Then, too, our struggle for existence has taken place largely in towns, where there is almost nothing to awaken any dormant love of nature. But, little by little, we are changing all that. Each year a larger portion of our city population is able to seek the refreshment and inspiration of the country during those months when it is almost, if not quite, at its loveliest. And while among this constantly in-

creasing class there are many, undoubtedly, who
"having eyes to see, see not," even among sights
sufficiently fraught with interest, one would suppose, to awaken the curiosity of the dullest, yet
there are others, many others, who can cry with
Mr. Norman Gale,

"And oh, my heart has understood
  The spider's fragile line of lace,
  The common weed, the woody space!"

who are quick to detect each bird-song, and eager
to trace it to its source; who follow curiously the
tiny tracks of the wood creatures; who note the
varied outlines of the forest leaves, and discover
the smallest of the flowers that grow beneath
them.

If we do not happen ourselves to be blessed
with a natural turn for observation, a little companionship with one of these more fortunate
beings will persuade us, I think, that the habit is
one which it would be both possible and desirable
to cultivate. It had never occurred to me, for example, that it would be worth while to look for
wild flowers on Fifth Avenue, until a certain
morning when a keen-eyed botanical companion
stooped and plucked from an earth-filled chink in
its pavement, a little blossom which had found its
way hither from some country lane. Since then I
have tried to keep my wits about me even on that
highway of the Philistines.

We are prone, most of us, to be inaccurate as well as unobservant; and I know of no better antidote to inaccuracy than a faithful study of plants. It is sometimes difficult for the flower-lover to control his impatience when he hears his favorites recklessly miscalled; and in this improving exercise he has ample opportunity to become proficient, for many people cling with peculiar tenacity and unreasonableness to their first erroneous impression of a flower's name. They consider anything so vague and poetic fair game for their ready imaginations, glibly tacking the name of one flower to another with inconsequential light-heartedness. Occasionally they have been really misled by some similarity of sound. Such was the case of an acquaintance of mine who persisted in informing the various companions of his rambles that the little pink-flowered shrub which blossoms in June on our wooded hill-sides was the sheep-sorrel; and refused to be persuaded that the correct title was sheep-laurel. His ear had caught the words incorrectly; but although this explanation was suggested, supplemented by the arguments that the laurel-like look of the flowers at once betrayed their lineage, and that the sheep-sorrel was the plant with halberd-shaped leaves and tiny clustered flowers which in spring tinges with red the grassy uplands, he would only reply with dignified decision that his conviction was based on trustworthy authority. So, perhaps, in at least one small circle, sheep-laurel is sheep-sorrel to this day.

But the uninitiated probably allow their imaginations to run more rife with the orchids than with any other flowers. Usually they are quite positive as to the general correctness of their conception of an orchid, and unless you are prepared to be made the object of a very genuine aversion, you will beware of trying to convince them of the error of their ways. In response to any such attempt they will defiantly challenge you: "Well, then, what *is* an orchid?" and woe betide you if you cannot couch your reply in half a dozen words of picturesque and unmistakable description. The term orchid is dear to their hearts. Whenever they discover a rare and striking flower they like to grace it with the title, and are sure to bear you a grudge for depriving them of the pleasurable power of conferring this mark of floral knighthood at will. Last year a friend of mine happened for the first time upon the lovely fringed polygala. Her delight in its butterfly beauty was unbounded. Having learned its name and studied its odd form she turned appealingly to me: "Could you *ever* call it an orchid?" she asked; and I was unpleasantly conscious of my apparent churlishness in refusing to ennoble, even temporarily, so exquisite a creation.

"I like flowers, but I hate to pull them to pieces," is the cry of the lazy nature-lover. Surely if we like a thing we wish to know something about it, to enjoy some intimacy with it, to learn its secrets. Who actually cares most for flowers, the man who glances admiringly at them and turns away, or he who studies their structure, inquires into the function of each part, reads the meaning of their marvellous coloring, and translates the invitation expressed by their fragrance? I doubt if he who has never been so brutal as "to pull a flower to pieces," even dimly understands all the strange, sweet joy of a wood walk, when we are tempted eagerly — almost breathlessly — but always reverently, with the reverence that is born of even the beginnings of knowledge, and by so much superior to that which springs from ignorance, to turn the pages and decipher what we can

"In nature's infinite book of secrecy."

When we learn to call the flowers by name we take the first step toward a real intimacy with them. An eager sportsman who had always noticed and wondered about the plants which he met on every fishing expedition, wrote to me a few weeks since that hitherto he had felt toward them as the charity-boy did about the alphabet, "he knew the little beggars by sight, but he couldn't tell their names"! And it has seemed as though a series of papers describing the different flowers to be found in the woods and fields, and by the road-sides, during the months suggested in their titles, might not only be helpful to those who care to "tell their names," but might increase the actual number of plants discovered, as one is far more likely to be successful in his search if he have a definite conception of what he can reasonably hope to find.

WINTER

—wide white fields, and fir-trees
capped with snow.

— BRYANT

During the winter I am content — or try to think I am — to make my head-quarters in town and to get fresh air and a broader outlook at intervals that are frequent, but still at intervals. Perhaps the walk or the drive out to the frozen lake among the hills for an afternoon's skating is the more keenly relished because of a busy week elsewhere. For all practical purposes nature is at a standstill. There is little chance that she will steal a march on me in the few days that intervene between my visits of inspection. And there is a wonderful joy in leaving behind the noisy city streets and starting out along the white road that leads across the hills. With each breath of the sharp, reviving air one seems to inhale new life. A peace as evident as the sunshine on the fields takes possession of one's inner being. The trivial cares which fretted like a swarm of mosquitoes are driven away by the first sweep of the wind that comes straight from the mountains. The graver anxieties seem to have dwindled in size as though in some unexplained way their proportions also were influenced by that same range of distant hills. Thoreau says that "many of our troubles are housebred." The tendency to magnify petty difficulties, to consider one's special problems impossible of solution, might be conquered, I believe, nine times out of ten, could we get out of doors and turn our attention to the impersonal but absorbing problems ready to present themselves to the open-eyed pedestrian. It is not possible always to run away from the routine of every-day life, but it is possible often when we fail to do it. The chances are that the thing we are striving to accomplish is not half so important or so inspiring as the thing that is crowded out. We may not think it wise "to postpone all to hear the locust sing," but I believe we should find more stimulus in association with our kind were we less weighted with the obligation to do an endless number of comparatively unimportant things.

One of the best botanists and ornithologists I know is a New York business man whose hours are long and whose work is exacting. But during his brief holidays and in the early morning he has seen sights and come to conclusions which have given him a high place in the estimation of his fellow-botanists and ornithologists. Few of us can anticipate such results, but with greater opportunities many of us might experience in some degree the joy of observation and investigation.

The time will come, I hope, when I can spend a whole year in the country. It is perfectly true that the contrast between town and country gives a flavor to both in turn that otherwise would be lacking. But unless on the spot all the year round the country-lover is sure to miss many events of importance. During the winter especially, when vegetable life is dormant and when animal life is infrequent, an occasional walk is likely to be poor in episodes of striking interest. In the books of John Burroughs and in Thoreau's journals I read enviously the winter notes on owls, partridges, red-polls, cross-bills, chickadees, and nuthatches, on mink, musk-rats, foxes, and squirrels. But even these brief lists covered not a single walk or a special day; they were the results of weeks of observation on the part of unusually keen observers.

For myself, almost the only birds that I see on my occasional country walks in winter are the crows. Perhaps because of this their cries as they reach my ear through the frozen silence sound pleasing and really musical. And I like to pause and watch them flap their deliberate way across the snowy fields, their jet-black bodies thrown in relief against the blue sky and the white hill-side.

Occasionally I discover a hawk circling high

overhead. Its slow, majestic evolutions are full of poetic grandeur. I feel sure the hawk exults in its own grace and power, it lingers so long and lovingly on its marvellous curves.

That chickadees, nuthatches, woodpeckers, even robins and bluebirds and a number of less common species are with us all or a part of the winter, as the books tell us, I do not doubt, but I rarely see any of them before March. In some sheltered spots they must wear out the nipping days and nights, venturing now and then into the barnyard or upon the doorstep for scattered grain or kindly crumbs and scraps.

Once or twice I have noticed a flock of juncoes in the city back-yard, driven to town, I suppose, for supplies. The only snow-bunting I ever saw was on West Forty-eighth Street, in New York City, where it had joined a group of English sparrows and was foraging in the gutter as contentedly as though it were not more at home in Arctic regions.

In the country in winter man seems to be almost as inactive as beasts and birds. If it were not for the smoke that drifts from its chimney the farm-house would appear deserted. Occasionally a sound of wood-chopping comes from the barn. Across the frozen pond the ploughman of last year guides his horse as he marks the ice for the winter harvest. Near the shore, his pronged sticks suspended over holes in the ice, the fisherman waits expectantly for pickerel. Here and there, with skates and sleds and eager young voices, the boys and girls add a touch of life to what seems almost like death. Occasionally a party of young people on skees transform a snowy hill-side into a scene of unrestrained gayety. A pine-bordered lake echoes the exultant cries of a group of skate-sailers, while along the neighboring river noise-lessly and triumphantly skim white-winged ice-boats. But these evidences of life are rare and in the nature of a surprise.

For the occasional visitor the value of the winter walk lies in his immediate surroundings. The intense silence that broods over the snow-bound land is a conscious blessing. The deep blue of the sky and the purple shadows cast by the trees and plants are a feast to the eye. The crunch of the snow-rind beneath his feet and the varied hum of the telegraph wires overhead are music to his ears.

Many of the oaks are rustling with leather-like leaves. I do not know why some of the oaks are well covered with dead leaves while others are almost naked. Thoreau claims that the young trees only retain their leaves, while he quotes Michaux as saying that this habit is peculiar to the white oak.

The pitch-pine, its rugged, spreading branches

holding great burdens of snow, is never so effective as at this season. The hemlocks and spruces also are strangely beautiful with their coating of snow, while the shrubs are hung with white garlands like a prophecy of spring.

An important part in the winter landscape is played by the dead grasses and other herbaceous plants, especially by various members of the composite family, such as the asters, golden-rods, and sunflowers. Wreathed in snow or incased in ice, they present a singularly graceful and fantastic appearance. Or, perhaps, the slender stalks and branches armed with naked seed-pods trace intricate and delicate shadows on the smooth snow.

The deciduous trees make an interesting winter study. At this season a tree lays bare its individuality. We note the angle at which its branches spring from the main trunk, the degree and direction in which these branches curve, the appearance of the bark, the arrangement of the buds, as we can at no other period of the year. It is something of an accomplishment as well as a pastime to be able to name correctly the leafless trees and shrubs as we drive along the road or flash by on the train.

The winter buds are a distinct stimulus to our lagging enthusiasm on days when spring seems too distant to be real. Each one is a promise to pay at an early date on which we can rely with confidence. The catkins of the alders are decorative as well as encouraging, decorative to an unusual degree after a storm when each little tassel enclosed in ice sparkles and quivers in the sunshine like a jewelled pendant.

Toward the latter part of winter even the unobservant become conscious of these winter buds. With the first mild days of February they swell and their color deepens. Especially in the uppermost ones, which receive the greatest share of sunshine, this is noticeable. The pulse quickens as we notice for the first time that the tree-tops on the wooded hill-side, gray and lifeless since November, are flushed with rosy color. The tops of the willows and the osiers are turning golden-yellow. The brambles and many other shrubs take on deep red and purple tints.

When the sun has melted the snow, or even where you push away the frozen crust, you are surprised to find the bright-green root-leaves of many plants that are not considered hardy, such as different members of the mustard family, chickweed, buttercup, speedwell, and others. Apparently they have profited by their icy covering.

Spring is in the cock's crow and in the dog's bark. It is in the fresh, stimulating odor that comes up from the earth, just bared to the sunshine. It is no longer wise for the nature-lover to procrastinate.

❧ 2 ❧

EARLY
GLIMPSES

In a pleasant spring morning all men's sins are
forgiven.

— THOREAU

E VEN SO FAITHFUL and experienced a watcher as Thoreau wrote: "No mortal is alert enough to be awake at the first dawn of spring." However eagerly we look each morning for the bursting of the earliest bud, or however zealously we listen for the actual song of the first bird, our bird or our flower, when it does come, is almost sure either to have been antedated by another, or to bear about it unmistakable evidence of having been on the scene for some days.

One of the first indications of the general awakening is given by the fallen keys of the maples. Before the last thin sheet of snow has melted, you see the maple-keys, or rather half-keys, for each pair is broken in two, standing erect, with uplifted wing, the seed-case usually burrowing its way into the earth before striking root. The seeds of two of our best-known maples, the red and the white, do not postpone their germination till the spring following their maturity, but often begin this work as soon as the keys have fallen. The early ripening of the fruit of these two species, which are the first to flower, secures the most favorable conditions for the speedy germination of their seed.

The bursting of the uppermost buds of these two maples, the pushing out of the catkins on the willows, poplars, alders, and birches, and the appearance in the swampy woods of the green, red, and purplish hoods of the skunk-cabbage are almost simultaneous, fresh signs that the year is carrying on her leisurely preparations for summer. Every hour now we expect some new evidence of her progress. The bee is ready to steal the pollen from the first tassel that turns yellow on the brook-loving willow. The pretty mourning cloak butterfly, its brown, velvety wings bordered with buff and spotted with blue, crawls out from the wood-pile into the sunshine. In the woods the chickadees, and in the gardens the juncoes, are chipping and chattering, while closely ranked, the cedar waxwings fly from one tree to another. All these are so-called winter birds, but to me they become frequent and conspicuous only in early spring.

These days, with what is almost homesickness,

I watch for the first robin. It is useless to look for him when the ground is covered with snow. But when the bare, brown earth comes through in great patches that are as fresh and sweet to the nostrils as they are welcome to the eyes, in some strange, unexplained fashion I am conscious that the robins have come. I never know just when and how this welcome and always thrilling discovery is made. Before I see them I feel them. Perhaps their voices reach me through the distance so faintly at first that I do not recognize fully their presence. But suddenly, without surprise, I hear close overhead that sharp clucking call, curiously human and suggestive of the anxious would-be householder. After a moment's search I see him high among the topmost, leafless branches of the elm. He stands motionless, his bright red breast shining in the sunlight. Then with another cluck-ing cry he flies away. Sometimes for a day or two he seems to be alone, but usually within fifteen minutes one or more of his fellows appear, with such an air of being at home that I feel sure they must have been on hand for several days. But whether or no this be the case matters little. With the coming of the first robin a peculiar elation possesses me. However blustering and snowy the March winds, they cannot fool me now. Youth and hope assert their eternal sway and melt the frozen rills of my being as surely as the sunshine is breaking up every brook that must find its way to the sea. The robin is not a rarity, but his advent makes the old man young again; for the moment it turns the dullard into a poet.

It may be some weeks before we hear the song of the robin, but this year I heard it during the latter half of March, within a few days of its first appearance. Its early morning call greeted my ears before I was fairly awake, and late in the afternoon, in heavy rain as well as in clear weather, the serene, melodious strain came to me from the tree-tops. It is a simple song but it is a beautiful one, speaking of faith and hope. There is an element of sadness about it which may be lent by the listener, I hardly know. But I do know that in all nature there is no sound which so swiftly takes one back to the happy, hopeful days of early life.

The bluebird, as compared with the robin, is a rarity in my neighborhood. It arrives usually a little later, and, though I have been on the watch for days, its blue, wavering flight and elusive song have always the effect of unexpectedness. It disappears as suddenly as it comes. Almost before I am sure it is here, out of sight it flashes. Till I have seen it for the second or third time I cannot be comfortably confident that the sudden vision is more than a dream. In my experience it lacks the aggressiveness and persistence which keep the robins with us, however unfriendly their environment. The robin is not to be driven from the neighborhood because of prowling cats, and barking dogs, and small boys with slings and a thirst for blood. Just as surely as the military ring in his voice assures you of his determination to stand up for his rights, the tremulous, confiding song of the bluebird expresses the doctrine of non-resistance. In this way there seems a sort of benediction in its companionship, a suggestion that the social atmosphere is charged with the "charity" and the "purity" which it preaches with such rare and persistent melody.

Almost simultaneously with the robins and bluebirds arrive the purple grackles. One welcomes them for what they represent rather than for what they are. Their plumage, with its iridescent blacks, greens, and purples, is beautiful, but their voices are strangely discordant, with the rusty creak of unoiled machinery. Occasionally in some note lurks a possibility of sweetness, but immediately it goes off into a discouraging squeak. Their manners also are rude and restless. We endure, however, even welcome, the grackles, because they are among the first heralds of spring.

The arrival of the song-sparrow, like that of the robin and bluebird, is among the uncertainties of the season. This little creature does not give vent at once to that strain of joyous confidence which later becomes so frequent. At first he hops stealthily about the bushes, lisping occasional sweet but hesitating notes, which we trace to their source with difficulty, if at all. As time goes on he gains boldness, and soon his gay little carol sounds from every quarter.

These are the days when we wait eagerly the passing of the fox-sparrow. Some windy March morning they are blown in upon us like an eddying gust of dead leaves. Then their song, the most complete and musical of the year so far, "a richly modulated whistle," seeming more like the perfect product of the mature year than the strain of some passing minstrel, reaches our delighted ears. For several days we watch them, plump, sparrow-like birds, with rich red-brown markings, scratching for seeds in the red-brown, leafless thicket. But one morning we stealthily approach their chosen feeding-ground, our ears alert for the fresh, airy, jubilant carol which has greeted us before, and all is silent. The fox-sparrows are on the way to their chosen resting-place in the far North.

If one quite ignorant of birds and their ways wishes to become better informed he should begin his ornithological studies during this month of March. In the first place, so few species are present that he is able with some degree of thoroughness and in a leisurely fashion to acquaint himself

WAKEROBIN

Trillium erectum

l

with the appearance and habits of one bird or species at a time. In the second place, at this season the trees and bushes are leafless, affording an almost unobstructed view of the birds that light on their branches, whereas later in the year the masses of foliage constantly interrupt our observations.

In April it becomes less easy to keep count of the new arrivals in the bird-world, for soon they reach us in great numbers. Now we may hope to hear the ecstatic, bubbling notes of the purple finch, the penetrating whistle of the peabody bird, the fine trill of the chipping sparrow, the spring-like call of the meadow-lark, and the varied songs of kinglets, vireos, warblers, and many others. But even though these additions are so rapid as to be confusing, the trees are still almost bare, and the lover of birds should be abroad constantly.

At times now the piping of the frogs is more noticeable than the bird-songs. Near a pond or close to marshy ground, just before sunset, the predominant sound is the shrill pipe of the hylas.

A very inconspicuous but significant sign of the season is found, after diligent search, in the branches of the hazel. Scarcely later than the maple-blossoms the little pistillate flower of this shrub ventures forth, "a crimson star, first dimly detected in the twilight," a star of the dawning rather than of the evening. Often I find at this same time the first faint-hued flowers of the liverwort and the early blossoms of the arbutus.

A dull-looking, uninteresting little plant, but one we ought to value because of the hardy persistence with which its silky leaves and yellowish flowers lighten the hill-sides when otherwise they are almost bare, is the plantain-leaved, or, as I have named it more to my satisfaction, the early everlasting.

The record of these first weeks of spring is not a full one. It seems to me that March and April, far more than May, love to

"— haggle with their greens an' things."

But Hosea Biglow is right in liking our "back'ard springs." They whet our appetite amazingly. The joy of realization is doubled by that of anticipation. I doubt whether the wealth of song and of blossom which delights us in June is worth more to us than the rare, suggestive notes that strike answering chords direct from our hearts, and the faint, unobtrusive flowers that meet our eyes one or two months earlier.

SPRING
IN THE CITY

The true harvest of daily life is somewhat as
intangible
and indescribable as the tints of morning or
evening.
— THOREAU

IN THE CITY as in the country there are marks of the changing seasons pregnant with suggestions to the nature-lover. One of the most unfailing season-marks in town is the turning on of the fountains in the public parks. How joyfully the liberated water flashes through the sunlit air. It seems to speak of the distant brooks that are released from bondage and free to ripple along their green-edged channels. There is a strange fascination about the sight and sound of water in motion. The sparrows dash with mad enjoyment in and out beneath the beaded, iridescent curves. The children pause in their play to watch, with wide, wondering eyes, the sparkling jets. Even the grown-up passers-by seem to fall under the spell and join the little group for a few wistful moments.

In the squares it seems as though in the space

of twenty-four hours the grass had changed from
dull brown to bright green. Here, too, we are
convinced of the arrival of spring by the blossoming trees. The great shining buds of the balm of
Gilead at last shake out their long tassels. The
upper gold-tinged branches of the white poplar
give a misty effect, which a careful inspection discovers to be due to a host of downy, close-set
catkins. The elms and maples let out tiny clusters
of red and yellow flowers — flowers so minute
and comparatively insignificant that if one is
caught, standing motionless, with head flung back,
and eyes upraised, and is able to account for his
apparently absurd attitude only by the explanation
that, Japanese-like, he is "viewing the blossoms,"
the chances are strong in favor of his being es-
teemed a harmless lunatic.

Another season-sign is afforded by the flower-
beds in these same squares. As soon as the frost is
fairly out of the ground, the needle-like tips of the
crocus appear. This plant is followed by tulip, hy-
acinth, and daffodil. But before they have time to
blossom, the vases that front the clubs and restau-
rants are filled with deep-hued pansies and English
daisies, the latter the cultivated variety of Burns's

"Wee, modest, crimson-tippit flower."

The florists' windows yield a veritable feast of
form and color. Even more of a delight are the
street flower-stands, and the moving gardens in

the shape of peddlers' flower-carts. These last seem like visions of a brighter world let into the dismal monotony of our dreary side-streets.

Strangely enough, few of these flowers which are peddled about the streets or sold in the shops, are natives. And as one studies the gayly filled window, or half unconsciously notes the contents of the peddler's cart, if he chance to be something of a traveller as well as a flower-lover, memories of many lands flash through his mind.

The yellow jonquils now so abundant recall the rocky shores of southern Italy, for during that wonderful drive from Castellamare to Sorrento, early in December (though properly and botanically these flowers belong to May), I first saw them at home. It has never been my good fortune to find in its native haunts that near cousin of the jonquil, the daffodil. But how abundant this is during the early spring in England no lover of Wordsworth need be told. And until he beholds it with other than the "inward eye," he has in possible anticipation an enchanting experience.

With the crocus is associated my earliest glimpse of Switzerland. It was already late in August when, for the first time, I looked upon the Alps. And almost as great as my awe-struck exultation in the grandeur of the snow-capped mountains was my delight in the green meadows at their feet, studded with the delicate blossoms of the fall crocus. A few days after this entrance into Switzerland, during a climb up one of the lower mountains, I found the lovely cyclamen, and soon learned to look upon this peculiarly satisfying flower, one of our most treasured importations, as the natural companion of my walks.

The little English daisy recalls a May morning at Hampton Court, where the smooth, grassy sweeps were starred with the dainty blossoms.

The close bunches of yellow primroses peddled at the street-corners, conjure up a vision of that quiet, high-banked flower-girt lane where perhaps we first heard the nightingale, where certainly, once and for all, we fell under the spell of the tranquil beauty of the mother-country.

One of our favorite Easter plants is the feathery white spiraea. This is a Japanese cousin of our well-known meadow-sweet and steeple-bush. The yellow genista, so abundant now, comes, I believe, from New Zealand. It suggests the wild indigo so common with us in summer, and also the English broom, all three of these plants being closely allied. The lovely foreign heaths, which look as though they came straight from the Scotch moors, could claim kinship with our trailing arbutus, our mountain-laurel, and with other favorite plants which belong to the same heath family.

Upon our avenues every sunny morning in early spring is found another season-mark which should not be overlooked. You could almost fancy that the floral decorations had not been confined

ROUND-LEAVED YELLOW VIOLET
Viola rotundifolia

to the squares, and to the grass-plots and vases that lie within the railings. All along the sidewalks, as far as the eye can reach, are patches of bright color. These bright patches are made by innumerable baby-carriages, whose gorgeous decorations harmonize in gay coloring with the pansies and daisies of the parks and window-boxes. And lovelier than either pansies or daisies are the little flower-faces that beam from the dainty equipages.

Another sign of the season is the call of "strawberries" from the street-venders. It is as full of suggestion as the first note of the bluebird. My journal last year records that I heard this call for the first time on the twenty-first; this year, I did not notice it till the fifth, about two weeks later; just as the birds and flowers are a fortnight later this year than last.

The English sparrows do their share in celebrating the return of spring. If in no other way, the intensified colors of the plumage of the males would signify that the period of courtship was at hand. But besides this, they are more obstreperous than ever; yet so joyfully obstreperous that I cannot find it in my heart to feel toward them all the antagonism that seems to be considered a mark of patriotism. That they never had been brought over to banish our far more attractive native birds is most heartily to be wished. But as they are with us, by no fault of their own, I find it impossible, especially at this season, to withhold from them a certain amount of sympathy. They are so overflowing with vitality, so brimful of plans, such ardent wooers, such eager house-builders. Their superfluous enthusiasm in this matter of house-building is responsible for the unsightly fringes of rope and other materials that decorate the under-eaves of our houses. The amount of energy that they throw into their slightest occupation shames our languid selves. And I frankly admit that I take a keen pleasure in seeing their palpitating little shadows sweep impetuously across the bars of sunlight that lie upon my floor. These seem to bring within the house something of the freedom of out-door life.

And to the city-bound lover of nature a peculiar satisfaction is yielded by the few objects which help to link his sympathies with his daily experience. That nightly certain stars sent into my room their far-reaching gaze seems to bring me into closer and more constant touch with the mysterious laws of the universe. These stars, too, are the most unfailing of all our season-marks, sky-flowers, "faithful through a thousand years." The stars which companion me these April nights are not those which glittered in the winter heavens. And by this silent march across my little limited patch of city sky, I am enabled to note the passage of the year more accurately than by any other of those indications which we, with city lives but country loves, look and long for each spring.

A SPRING HOLIDAY

I, country-born an' bred, know where to find
Some blooms thet make the season suit the mind,
An' seem to metch the doubtin' blue-bird's notes, —
Half-vent'rin' liverworts in furry coats,
Bloodroots, whose rolled-up leaves ef you oncurl,
Each on 'em's cradle to a baby-pearl, —
But these are jes' Spring's pickets; sure ez sin,
The rebble frosts 'll try to drive 'em in;
For half our May's so awfully like May'nt,
'T would rile a Shaker or an evrige saint;
Though I own up I like our back'ard springs
Thet kind o' haggle with their greens an' things,
An' when you 'most give up, 'ithout more words
Toss the fields full o' blossoms, leaves, an' birds.

— LOWELL

THE COUNTRYMAN can hardly know the heart-swell and the pulse-throb which comes to the city-prisoned man or woman who breaks bounds after months of abstinence and feasts on the first evidences of returning life in the woods and fields. Spring glides gradually into the farmer's consciousness, but on us city people it bursts with all the relish of a sudden surprise, compensating for much of what we lose.

One day last week we resolved to break away from work and take a brief, unexpected vacation. So, early the next morning, breathless but happy, we watched the city blocks becoming more and more diluted, first with sordid vacant spaces, receptacles for nameless rubbish, attesting man's tendency to acquisitiveness and his depraved liking for embalmed vegetables and refreshments abhorred of teetotalers, then with incipient gardens, restoring one's lost faith in humanity, and finally with miniature farms, gradually blending into actual fields bounded by gray hill-sides.

Spring is really behind time this year. And when one is behind time himself, this accommodation of the season fills him with satisfaction. At times on this particular morning the woods looked so bare and lifeless that it seemed as though winter were trying to lap over into May. The ground in places was thickly matted with dead leaves, while here and there, in a depression in the woods or on the sides of the hills, lay a patch of dirty snow.

But part of this wintry aspect was due to town eyes, used to the crude masses and sharp outlines of city buildings. Soon the woods were seen to be blurred faintly as though looked at through a mist. We noticed that the outlines of many of the branches were broken, in most cases by innumerable clusters of tiny flowers, these usually without the more vivid coloring of later blossoms. The flowers of the swamp-maple formed an exception to this rule. This tree fringed the woods with the vivid scarlet of its myriad blossoms, and lightened the low-lying swamps almost as its dying leaves lighten them in October. Another exception was seen in the flowers of the male willows, which sent out stamens heavy with yellow pollen that turned the catkins into golden tassels, and made these willows conspicuous in the swamps and along the streams.

The elms along the railway were not yet in leaf, but looked as though wreathed in a coppery mist — an effect due to the minute blossoms which appear before the leaves put out. The sugar-maples were bursting into leaf and flower simultaneously. Some weeks ago the birches hung out their yellow catkins, and now their branches were blurred with delicate foliage. This was especially noticeable with the white birches, clustering erect and slim on the mountain-sides.

The oaks, still hung with the leathery leaves of last year, the hickories, chestnuts, and, indeed, most of the trees we could identify, showed few signs of coming summer. But their dull grays and browns blended with the misty greens, reds, and yellows of maple, birch, and willow, forming a landscape full of tender beauty.

We passed fields velvety with the "unnamed green" of new-sprung winter rye; then skirted the base of a hill-side red with upturned soil, whose fresh, earthy scent seemed almost to reach us through the smeared window-panes. We watched, touched by envy born of inexperience, the farmer guiding his plough in the pale sunlight with the skill that makes the hardest work look easy. Across another fresh-ploughed field strode a sower, strong and sinewy, with swinging, easy motion; and we wondered if the brown, solitary figure against the hazy background would have seemed equally full of poetry and suggestion had we never seen Millet's painting.

We flashed by a bank recently burned over, so that no shrubs or débris obscured its fresh growth. From the black slope, star-like, gem-like, distinct and symmetrical, sprang the delicate flowers of the liverwort, recalling vividly one of the Fra Angelico foregrounds.

We crossed a swamp where bright marsh-marigolds huddled together on little islands. In the woods beyond, the huge leaves of the skunk-cabbage made patches of bright green. As a native foliage-plant the skunk-cabbage is surpassed only by the false hellebore, whose fresh-looking many-plaited leaves were just unfolding in these same woods.

One of the most satisfying features of the ride was the constant companionship of brooks big and little, brooks that ran full and swift, with the repletion of melting snows and the sparkle of a spring morning. Watching these brooks, the old trite expressions forced themselves into one's mind — "unlocked," "unbound," "laughing," "babbling," "chattering." From time immemorial man has loved these overflowing brooks, and has tried, not altogether without success, to interpret their inevitable charm.

PAINTED TRILLIUM
Trillium undulatum

The day was still young when we reached the town where we were to mount our wheels and cross the intervening hills to the inn which was our destination. As we sped down the long white road the last remnant of care slipped from us and we abandoned ourselves completely to the pure joy of swift motion and bounding blood. I say completely, but I am wrong, for, even when coasting down a hill, the sliding, misty, sun-bathed landscape is part of one's consciousness; and so are the shrill-voiced frogs, the lisping, uncertain birds, and the butterflies that chase each other into the sky for the mere fun of the thing.

And when we were not coasting down a hill, but pursuing a fairly moderate pace along a level road, we noted even the details of the wayside, contrasting the silver-green catkins of the fertile willows with the golden tassels of the sterile, ex-ulting in the glossy green limbs of the speckled alder, guessing at the circumference of the great elm which marks a turn in the road, sympathizing with the yellow-haired children who had brought out into the sunlight their tailless wooden horses and their ragged dolls, for joy of the perfect morning.

Then came a hill too steep to climb save on foot, affording a chance to peer over the stone wall and wonder why this part of the world was so backward, and if all the flowers were left behind on the cinder-bank. Another ride on a fine level path, beneath shadowy, blue-green pines, and another climb, this time without dismounting. Then a rest (and, unless you have forced your bicycle up a hill under the morning sun, you don't know the meaning of that word) beneath a blossoming elm, seeking the shadow of its trunk, for the leafless branches gave little protection, staring lazily into the swamp beneath, bright with its willows and maples, and at the dim mountains beyond. So finally we reach our destination, with excellent appetites for an excellent dinner, and a strong tendency afterward to loaf indefinitely about the pretty village.

But at last we summoned the energy necessary for a fresh start, on foot this time, for some neighboring woods. The road led through a pine-grove, then by a grassy opening, beyond which, on a rocky slope beneath deciduous trees which let down great squares of sunlight, grew the starry, white-petaled, yellow-centred flowers of the bloodroot, each one partially encircled by its pale, protecting leaf. It was some time before we could take our fill of these snowy beauties. One had to get fairly down on the ground to appreciate their delicate perfection, for their whole ethereal aspect forbids handling.

Now the floor of the forest became matted with dead leaves. It was only by keeping close watch of every glimpse of green that, within two minutes after leaving the bloodroot behind us, we discovered the thick, somewhat rusty leaves, and the flowers, wax-like and spicily fragrant, of the trailing arbutus. Within a limited area the plant grew abundantly, its blossoms, now pure white, again delicately pink, sometimes exposing themselves freely to the sunlight, and seeming to give out their fragrance the more generously for its warmth, but oftener hiding beneath the dead, fallen leaves. I denied myself the pleasure of picking more than one or two sprays of these flowers, singularly tempting though they were, so fearful am I of the extermination of this plant, the especial pride, perhaps, of our spring woods, and the peculiar object of the cupidity of ruthless flowerpickers.

Beyond the haunt of the arbutus, springing from a ledge which overlooked a valley lovely in the greens and grays of the early year, we found the white, slender-petaled flowers of the shadbush. Here, too, were young, silky fronds of that interesting little fern, the rusty woodsia. And here we flung ourselves on the dry, fragrant pineneedles, and listened to the wind blowing through the pines overhead and across the tree-tops below, and forgot that holidays ever came to an end.

Now the road climbed a hill where the trees, other than the evergreens, became more and more leafless and flowerless, and where the young plants dwindled into earliest infancy, showing little more than tiny spears of green. The white-veined partridge-vine, thickly studded with bright berries, and the little wintergreen, whose hanging red balls are flavored with so delicious an essence of the woods, did their best to cover the deficiency of other undergrowth, climbing over the roots of trees and carpeting the forest hollows with cheerful persistency. But when we descended toward the valley beyond, close to a little stream that trickled down the hill-side, we found the crinkle-root quite full grown, its three-divided leaves large and fresh, and its white, cress-like flowers almost expanded. We dug up a bit of its fleshy woodstock and nibbled it from time to time, fancying that its pungent woodland flavor added a new relish to our holiday.

Still more interesting was the discovery of the showy orchis, even though the flower-spike, pushing up between two great oblong shining leaves, needed a few more warm days for its unfolding. This is a quaint, somewhat rare little plant, very charming when its clustered pink-and-white flowers are in full bloom. Then, too, it is generally acknowledged to be the first orchid of the year to flower, a fact which entitles it to special consideration.

Close to the plants of the showy orchis grew the rattlesnake fern (*Botrychium virginianum*) in various stages of development. *Botrychium* is not a true fern, and consequently its young frond does not curl up in conventional "fiddle-head" fashion, but folds over the fertile portion, which is also "doubled up" in the bud. In its immediate neighborhood, however, there was no lack of "fiddle-heads."

The interrupted fern and the cinnamon fern had just come up "fist first," and could easily be identified by their juicy, vigorous appearance, and by their soft wrappings of white or brownish wool. In sunny, sheltered spots they had thrown aside their wraps, and were erecting, gracefully enough, their slender, pale-green fronds. Many other species, less warmly clothed, yet chiefly distinguishable by the brown or black or whitish scales of the young fronds, were shooting up on every side, now curled into the smallest possible compass, watch-spring fashion, and now almost erect, though still noticeable for a certain scrawny youthfulness of aspect. But the day was waning, and we were obliged to leave further explorations till the next morning if we hoped for any tea that night.

The next day dawned bright and clear. We mounted our wheels, and made our destination some woods of quite a different character from those we had visited the day before. They were low-lying and, in places, swampy. Before leaving the open we visited the banks of a tiny brook, whose green, inviting shores suggested pleasant possibilities. Here we found our first violets — little yellow ones, the so-called "downy" species, growing in fresh clumps. Near by, on erect, leafless stems, looking like a dandelion with its heart plucked out, we discovered the coltsfoot, otherwise the "coughwort," "clay-weed," "horse-foot," and "hoofs." This being the first time I had ever found this plant in flower, the occasion was memorable.

A wet, mossy rock looked as though it might harbor any number of plant-waifs. Picking my way along the slippery banks, I shouted with joy on seeing, lovely, fresh, and dainty, springing airily from the flattened top, the first liverworts we had found since leaving the train the previous morning. In the chinks of this same rock were soft young clusters of the fragile bladder-fern, still immature, but exquisitely green and promising. On the farther side of the rock grew that odd-looking plant, the blue cohosh, sometimes called "papoose-root,' with smooth, purplish stem, purple, divided leaves, and clusters of purple flowers. Close to this plant was a leafless shrub with insignificant yellow blossoms, and bark so tough that it was almost impossible to break off a branch. This proved to be the "leatherwood" used by the Indians for thongs. It is also known as "moosewood" and "swampwood."

Once more on our wheels along the winding road and we were in the woods again. In the spring woods the sun filters everywhere through the leafless branches, and nowhere did it meet lovelier upturned flower-faces than here, where myriad, many-hued blossoms of the liverwort expanded beneath its rays. Never before had I seen this flower so abundant and so perfect — pure white, pale lavender, deep violet, or pink of the most delicate shade. I abandoned my usual principle of leaving flowers as I find them, and I gathered them recklessly, with exultant, extravagant joy, seeking every little variety of shade, selecting the largest and most complete specimens, fairly gloating over their perfection of delicate beauty. Though the individual flowers of the liverwort are hardly fragrant, a faint and delicious odor came from the great bunch which finally I held.

While hunting these beauties I stumbled over a patch of yellow adder's-tongue, its delicate lily-like flowers nodding between the smooth, mottled leaves. Already I had found patches of these leaves, but nowhere else the plant in blossom. Close by, the little bellwort hung out its pale, straw-colored blossom.

During a drive over the mountain in the afternoon we noticed the white flowers of the saxifrage bursting from almost invisible crevices in the rocks in its usual sturdy, attractive fashion. Many of the plants were so young that the flower-cluster, pinkish in bud, was still sunk deep in the rosette of leaves.

At breakfast the next morning there was a noticeable tendency to the "blues," indicating that our holiday was nearly over. But once a-wheel in the crisp morning air the joy of living came back with unabated strength, and, as our course lay mostly down hill, the ride was peculiarly invigorating. Now, too, our holiday did as a well-behaved holiday should, keeping the best for the last. We had allowed more time than necessary for this ride, that we might explore a tempting piece of woods close to the town where we were to take the train. Nothing that we had seen since leaving home equalled those woods. First the usual mat of dead leaves, then liverwort and yellow adder's-tongue in the sunny spaces, then great bowlders with lovely little forest gardens on their flat surfaces; the young woolly leaves of the wild ginger, its bell-like, red-brown, shamefaced flower actually pretty in its freshness; great groups of wake-robin with gay purple-red blossoms catching the sunlight; tiny bellworts, and the bursting, purplish blossoms and delicate foliage, suggestive of maidenhair, of the early meadow-rue. Still farther in were receding cliffs with moss-grown shelves harboring feathery tufts of bladder-fern, and — their crowning glory — great soft masses of the finely cut leaves of the

COLTSFOOT
Tussilago farfara

squirrel-corn, with here and there a spike of pale-pink, heart-shaped flowers. The moments flew, and the hour when we must meet our train was perilously near. With one long look we left our beautiful woods, remounted our wheels, and resolved to live the week through on fragrant memories.

❧ 5 ❧

MAY NOTES

The world hangs glittering in star-strown
space,
Fresh as a jewel found but yesterday.
— T. B. ALDRICH

$\mathcal{A}$s our seasons vary from year to year, a fair degree of latitude must be granted anyone who attempts to classify either flowers or birds "according to season." But usually the same flowers are contemporaneous. When I find the liverwort in blossom, I begin to look for the bloodroot and the adder's-tongue. In some sunny hollow the delicate pink-tinged and striped stars of the spring beauty are almost expanded. And before many days have passed the tremulous blossoms of the two anemones will quiver with the least breath of wind, as they nestle among the great roots of the forest trees.

In my neighborhood the columbine blossoms occasionally before the end of April, yet it may fairly be considered a May flower. In favorable exposures it appears early in the month, while on the hills it is hardly in its prime till the latter part. Its pendant blossoms, with protruding yellow stamens, and curved, spur-like petals, red without and yellow within, showing vividly against their soft background of delicate foliage, are associated with the pale young leaves, just beginning to expand, of neighboring maples and birches.

To this period belongs the downy yellow violet, a flower which seems almost a part of the sunshine that filters plentifully into the depths of the thickest woods these May days. Yet I doubt if the downy yellow is the first of its tribe to blossom. The flowers of the round-leaved violet, another yellow species, are among the early arrivals, and I suspect that they antedate their congeners. The books assign both alike to "April-May." But I have found the flowers of the round-leaved fading while those of the downy were still erect and fresh.

The round-leaved is something of a recluse. It likes to withdraw itself to unfrequented woods. In its leaves lie its greatest individuality. These heart-shaped leaves are not especially conspicuous when the plant is in flower. But later in the year they broaden by two or three inches, lying flat on the ground, and presenting a shining surface which readily attracts the eye.

The two yellow species are followed closely by the common blue violet. In the manner of its growth, the shape of its leaves, and the color of its flowers, this little plant shows a tendency to whims. It might readily be taken for half a dozen different species on as many occasions. But, whimsical or not, it is one of our best-loved flowers. It links itself with our earliest recollections. Fair and slender it grew beneath the pink-and-white blossoms of the old orchard, among the long grasses of the neighboring swamp, close to eager, childish feet, along the lane. With a deeper purple it covered the little mossy islands in the beloved brook, that flashed and hummed its way beneath spreading clusters of the hobble-bush and drooping racemes of the mountain maple. But, perhaps, after all, we loved it best for the fidelity and tenderness with which it brightened otherwise waste and barren spots. Every year these blue violets sprang up in the neglected corners of the back-yard. They carpeted the desolate banks of the railway before it had cleared the suburbs, where otherwise only the coarsest and rankest of weeds made themselves at home. They ran rife in the old graveyard

"where like an infant's smile over the dead
A light of laughing flowers along the grass
    is spread."

Blossoming at the same time as the common blue violet, I find the dog violet. This is a low, branching plant, with leafy stems that easily distinguish it from the common blue violet, which bears it flowers singly on naked stems.

The long-spurred violet, another species with leafy stems, as well as with pale lilac flowers that are noticeably long spurred, is assigned by the botanists to June and July, but it is on my May list and I find it flowering with the other early species.

Perhaps the least showy of the group is the sweet white violet. This attractive little plant grows abundantly in our wet woods, permeating the immediate neighborhood with its faint, sweet fragrance. With it we find frequently the lance-leaved species, bearing flowers that are similar to *V. blanda,* but with erect, narrow leaves, quite unlike the rounded, heart-shaped ones of its kinsman.

A strikingly handsome, and to me more unusual, member of the family is the bird's-foot violet. Its blossom is velvety and pansy-like, often with one or both of the upper petals of a darker shade. Its leaves are deeply divided into narrow lobes. Before the Botanical Gardens came into being I used to find it bordering the Bronx River. The 11th of May last, during a drive along the north shore of Long Island, on the sandy banks by the road-side, the more fresh and lovely because little else seemed to flourish there, I saw it flowering in abundance.

LONG-SPURRED VIOLET
Viola rostrata

A near relative of our wild violets, the garden pansy, occasionally strays beyond its garden walls and makes itself at home along the public highway.

At the same time, and in much the same soil and region as harbors the bird's-foot violet, we look for the bright flowers of the wild-pink. These never seem to me more attractive than when they flash into sight as we drive or travel by rail. In the hand they lack the delicacy of finish and detail which we find in so complete and satisfactory a flower as the violet.

Two distant relations of the early saxifrage, the foam-flower and the mitrewort, are abundant in the May woods. The first is well named. Its small white flowers are massed in soft clusters which spot the woods like flecks of foam. Its lobed, heart-shaped leaves spring direct from the root, with the occasional exception of one or two leaves which rarely appear upon the stem. But the delicate, crystal-like blossoms of the mitrewort, so small that we need a microscope to see them properly, are more suggestive of snow-flakes than of mitres. Their slender, wand-like clusters are easily overlooked among their more showy companions. The root-leaves of the mitrewort are not unlike those of the foam-flower. The two stem-leaves are opposite.

Perhaps we look upon certain plants as rarities because we did not happen to know them in childhood, the period when events make the strongest impression. The flowers I found as a child rarely seem to me unusual, while many of those I have learned to know well in later life are possessed of a certain permanent novelty. One of these more recent acquaintances is the fringed polygala. Since I found it for the first time a few years ago, springing fresh and frail in its butterfly beauty above the dead leaves, it has been one of the frequent prizes of my May pilgrimages. Yet I never become altogether accustomed to its delicate charm. The expedition which it brightens is necessarily a success. During a drive across some lonely hills lying near the upper shores of the Hudson, the road-side was carpeted for miles by the tender, just expanded leaves and dainty, purplish-pink flowers of this little plant. I had never seen it growing in such profusion, yet neither then nor later did it become a matter of course. It is to be wished that the fringed polygala had been blessed with a godfather more sensitive to sound. Its English name lends itself to parody. A light-minded friend has christened it "fringed polygamy." It is not unlikely that this title will descend to posterity in that misguided family.

To these hills which harbored so abundantly the fringed polygala I owe my first acquaintance with the painted trillium. In describing the early flowers one needs to keep a tight rein on one's adjectives. At this season, not every flower, but pretty nearly every other flower, is possessed of a charm so individual, so convincing, that for the moment we are inclined to yield it supremacy. I remember that this especial day the pink-striped stars of the painted trillium shining through the misty, ineffable green of the spring woods, seemed to pale into momentary insignificance less conspicuous blossoms. They were growing near a lake of considerable extent which had fairly earned its title of "crooked." In and out of the many bends of this lake I was walking with the intention of making the complete circuit. Till I found the painted trillium I had persevered in my resolve not only to leave intact the fresh perfection of the woods, but to keep myself unhampered for a difficult tramp. But those painted trilliums proved too much for me. In their sudden presence every resolution dissolved. I fell upon them as ruthlessly, as flower-thirstily, as though I had never bored my friends with dissertations on loving the rose and leaving it on its stalk. Many were the headless trillium stalks which met my furtive eyes. But later they had their revenge. The great, gay bunch proved a growing burden. At last, in a shamed, stealthy fashion, with something of the sense as well as the appearance of one who conceals the fruit of his dark crime, I hid the drooping, recklessly gathered blossoms behind a pile of dead underbrush, comforting myself as best I could with a vague and futile, though scarcely misleading, assurance that I might regain them later.

The May flower-hunt is not always attended with such interesting if not unusual discoveries as fringed polygalas and painted trilliums. But even though the neighborhood be comparatively unfamiliar or unpromising, usually we count upon certain flowers. In low, moist places we find, as we have found for more years than we can remember, the purple or green-veined canopies of Jack-in-the-pulpit. Probably side by side we notice those faithful companions, the true and the false Solomon's seal, the former bearing its greenish, somewhat fragrant flowers in a terminal plume, the latter with small, straw-colored bells hanging from the under side of its curved, leafy stem. Frequently in the same neighborhood and with a strong family likeness grow one or both of its kinsmen, the twisted stalks, one with pink, the other with greenish-white, bell-like flowers. Another familiar member of this lily family is the little *Maianthemum*. This plant is without an English name, unless we accept the vague title, applied, I find, indiscriminately to different plants, of "wild lily of the valley." More noticeably a lily than any of these others, is the *Clintonia*, another plant as yet unnamed except by the botanist. Its handsome, oblong leaves, large and shining, and its clustered, lemon-colored flowers abound in the cool, mountainous woods of the North. Though I believe the plant grows as far south as North Carolina, I say of the North because in the woods of the Adirondacks and of Maine I find it most abundantly. Frequently the *Clintonia* does not live up to its possibilities, but when it bears its full complement of leaves and flowers, four leaves and seven (I believe) blossoms being the greatest number I have found on a single plant, it is noticeably beautiful. At such a time in general effect it suggests the yellow adder's-tongue (*Erythronium*) which borders the snow-fields and glaciers of the Canadian Rockies.

Many other lovers of the deep northern woods grow with the *Clintonia*. From its whorl of delicate pointed leaves springs the pure blossom of the star-flower. Frequently the ground is carpeted with the glossy three-divided leaves and small white flowers of the gold-thread, whose name we readily understand if we take up a handful of the dark moist earth which is threaded with its orange-colored roots. The pure inflorescence of the bunch-berry borders the wood-paths and fills many of the open spaces where the woods have been cut or burned away. Often with its companions, the *Clintonia*, twisted stalk, and *Maianthemum*, it leaves the more inland woods, and ventures far down on shaded rocky points that jut into the sea.

It is not easy to say whether the pink lady's-slipper or Indian moccasin belongs more properly to May or to June. According to the latitude and the year it may be found in flower at any time from the middle of the earlier to the end of the later month. Thoreau writes, "The first of June, when the lady's-slipper and the wild pink have come out in sunny places on the hill-side, then the summer is begun according to the clock of the seasons." But it seems to me to range itself more naturally with the spring than with the summer flowers, and in like manner to belong to the northern woods. The natural background for its striped, pinkish pouch, swinging balloon-like from the tall stem which is guarded by two broad, curving leaves, is the leafy red-brown carpet beneath the pines, hemlocks, and spruces. Different and almost discordant as the purple pink of the flower might seem in combination with the rich, reddish hue of the forest floor, yet in reality the two shades not only harmonize, but blend so perfectly that the flower, large and conspicuous though it is, frequently is overlooked by the passer-by. Undoubtedly this is due in part to the reddish coloring of the narrow, waving sepals and petals which in comparison to the great inflated lip are inconspicuous parts of the flower. Perhaps this is an example of the protective mimicry which may exist as well in the vegetable as in the animal world. The plant stands sorely in need of some such device to shield it from the attack of the omnipresent flower-picker. More than once I have held my breath and looked the other way while passing with a companion one or more of these flowers. That they are appreciated very generally and destructively is proved by the fact that they are gathered in quantities, tied up in close, uncomfortable bunches, and sold from the carts that fill the open market-place in Albany on early May mornings. Occasionally the flower loses its color and becomes either a bleached or, very rarely, a pure white. Once only I have found it entirely white with yellow-green sepals and petals, and so tall stemmed and large-leaved as to look like quite a different species.

The two yellow lady's-slippers, the larger and the smaller species, are usually a few days later than the Indian moccasin. Gray assigns them to "bogs and low woods," but I happen to have found them only on rather dry, wooded hill-sides. They are interesting and pretty plants, less frequently met with than the pink species.

A May orchid which I have not yet found growing in this part of the world is *Calypso borealis*. This lovely little plant is essentially northern, having been found, so far as I know, only in

Maine, New Hampshire and Vermont, of the New England States. But early one June I had the good-luck to see it flowering on the lower slopes of the Canadian Rockies, though unfortunately the majority of the blossoms had been plucked from the plants in order to decorate the tables of the hotel dining-room at Banff. Its pouch, purple or pinkish in color, shading below into yellow, and tufted with yellow hairs, suggests a small lady's-slipper.

The great, white, waxlike flower of the May-apple, which blooms at this season, is so beautiful and so common that one hardly knows why it does not hold the place in our imagination to which its good looks would seem to entitle it. The long-stemmed, glossy, umbrella-like leaves which hide it from view till we push them aside are sufficiently striking and handsome to attract our notice without any aid from the blossom. Earlier in the month, before they began fairly to open out, each one of these leaves looked as though a finger were pushing up against it from below with such force as to drive the blood from the finger-tip. Perhaps the comparative unpopularity of the flower is due in part to its rather unpleasant odor, in part to its short stems which will not permit it to be made up into bunches, while, if it is picked with the leaves, not only is it hidden entirely from view, but the leaves fade almost immediately.

CORN-LILY
Clintonia borealis

Though a wood-loving plant, it is rather the inhabitant of wood-borders than of the deeper forest.

Another lover of the open woods is the wild-geranium. This flower varies greatly in color, being spoken of sometimes as blue, again as purple, again as pink. Its usual color seems to me most accurately described as lavender.

Toward the latter part of the month, the blue, or, more properly, the purple flag tinges the meadows with royal color. It seems truly "born to the purple." I do not sympathize with Thoreau's feeling that it is "loose and coarse in its habit," "too showy and gaudy, like some women's bonnets." The blue-eyed grass is another flower which is perhaps misnamed, being more purple than blue. But its title is so pretty, and, save for the color mentioned, so appropriate, that we gladly overlook its inaccuracy. In grassy fields we notice the thick, close tufts of its delicate, yellow-centred blossoms. When the sun disappears, or if they are picked, the little "blue" eyes close.

A flower of this season that may fairly be described as blue is the lupine. It grows usually in sandy, somewhat open places, where little else flourishes, with long, bright clusters of pea-like blossoms that make the hill-side seem a reflection of May skies.

An odd and, with me, somewhat unusual little

plant, which may be found flowering in damp woods at this season, is the cancer-root. It is a parasite, living on the roots of other plants, and its leafless, lurid yellow stems are crowned with a rather pretty lavender-colored flower which resembles a violet.

The different shades of yellow are abundant now. It is not easy to understand the spirit which moved Wordsworth, that faithful celebrant of the "unassuming commonplace," to write

> "Ill befall the yellow flowers
> Children of the flaring hours."

The spring would lose something of its joy if its consummation were not blazoned in our consciousness by the gold of the dandelions. Their lovely constellations make a little heaven on earth of the grassy places that have been brown and bare for months. The first dandelions touch the heart-strings in much the same way as do the early notes of the robin, their blessed familiarity impressing us like a happy surprise.

The slender strands of the little cinquefoil carpet the meadows and road-sides, its divided leaves deluding the average passer-by into the belief that it is a yellow-flowered wild-strawberry. In moist ditches we notice the flat-tipped clusters of the early meadow-parsnip, suggesting its kinship to the wild-carrot of summer. Certain meadows, especially southward, are flooded with deep orange. If we explore them we discover the deep-hued flower-heads, somewhat suggesting dandelions, of the cynthia. More generally abundant, perhaps, is the golden ragwort, with much the aspect of a yellow daisy. The various yellow members of the mustard family begin also to be abundant. Most of these are coarse, rank-growing plants, but with flowers that in their prime wear a pure and lovely yellow.

Of the native trees which flower in May, one of the smallest, but perhaps the most beautiful, is the dogwood. Its flat, spreading branches look as though laden with drifts of snow. The inflorescence of this tree is similar to that of its little relation, the bunch-berry, each apparent flower consisting of a close cluster of small greenish blossoms, which are surrounded by pure white, showy, petal-like leaves. Occasionally these petal-like leaves are pink. The only pink dogwood I remember to have seen was growing in a lane near the Bronx River some years ago. Whether it is still standing I do not know. But I shall always carry in my mind a picture of its rosy loveliness as it flung its spreading pink-wreathed branches across the lane, feathery with young green things and bordered with columbines, bellworts, wild-ginger, Dutchman's breeches, and other flowering plants whose exact identity I do not recall.

The white clusters of the wild-cherry-trees

lighten the hill-sides. Along the country lanes droop the slender racemes of the choke-cherry. Among the later maples to flower are the striped and the mountain species. The mountain-maple is a tall shrub, easily identified by its erect clusters of greenish flowers, which, later in the year, are replaced by vivid pink-tinged fruit. The striped species is a small tree which owes its name to its light bark, which is streaked with dark lines. It bears its greenish flowers in loose, drooping racemes. In some places it is known as "moosewood."

Perhaps more actually decorative effects are secured by the shrubs that flower in May than by either the trees or the smaller plants. One of the earliest of these is the red-berried elder, with its pyramidal masses of white blossoms. Along the lanes the thorns are conspicuous. In their white, round-petalled flowers with pink-tipped stamens we see evidences of their kinship to the apple-blossoms. Deep in the woods, often throwing its picturesque, straggling branches across some swift-rushing stream, we find the flat clusters of the hobble-bush.

The Labrador tea is blossoming in these same woods, though more abundantly far northward, as its name indicates. The individuality of this shrub is always interesting on account of the leathery leaves which are heavily lined with rust-colored wool, suggesting ample protection against cold and wet. On this hardy-looking plant it is a surprise to find the delicate, somewhat fragrant white blossoms.

Far less frequent than the white-flowered shrubs in May are those with colored blossoms. Yet this is the month of the pink azalea, which grows in great tangles in the wet meadows, creeping with warm waves of color into every little bay formed by the dark promontories of the neighboring woods. A shrub nearly related to the azalea, which I never found in flower till this year, is the rhodora. For the first time I was able to visit its haunts early enough to see the brilliant butterfly-blossoms, purplish-pink in color, almost blotting out of sight the framework of the shrub. The thrill of excitement caused by this experience was not due, perhaps, so much to my admiration of its beauty or appreciation of its, to me, unusualness, as to the interest inspired by the flower which had moved Emerson to write one of his loveliest poems.

In May the birds become so numerous that it would be impossible to describe any great number of them in a book not devoted to the subject. For many birds May is the most important month of the year, for it is their time of nesting. Their song now approaches its greatest perfection. Early in the month it expresses the rapture of courtship, later the joy of possession.

From swampy meadows come the gurgling notes of the red-winged blackbirds, whose bright shoulder-bars flash above the gleaming grasses. The cat-bird mews within the shrubbery that skirts the lawn. Under the eaves of the barn the cliff-swallows take possession of their curious bottle-like nests, which have done service from year to year. The barn-swallows prefer to go inside and build upon the rafters, while the tree-swallows look out for holes in trees and posts. On or near the ground in swampy thickets the Maryland yellow-throat builds its nest, while from the forked branch of some low tree the red-eyed vireo hangs its cup-like cradle.

May is the month of the oriole. In and out among the apple-blossoms and lilacs and other gay-flowered garden shrubs, rivalling, if not surpassing their brilliant colors, it flashes in its search for food and for material with which to build its swinging home in the elm-tree. Its penetrating whistle possesses much the same quality for the ear as its flame-like color does for the eye.

If the oriole is the bird of the orchard and garden, the upland meadows belong to the bobolink. All the joy of life these spring days is in its tinkling song. A rapture of abandonment, a veritable tintinabulation of glee, comes up to us from those deep floods of grass and flowers. When in his wedding-coat of black and white, I know no such interpreter of pure lightheartedness as the bobo-link. Once this is laid aside, he seems to feel, "the heavy and the weary weight," like the rest of us.

The wood-thrush is the bird of the May woods. Early in the month I hear for the first time his serene, hymn-like notes. However commonplace my actual surroundings may be, instantly I am transported to

"some melodious plot
Of beeches green and shadows
numberless,"

and my whole being is permeated with the spirit of perfect serenity, of which this song is the apotheosis.

6

"THE LEAFY MONTH OF JUNE"

Now is the high-tide of the year,
  And whatever of life hath ebbed away
Comes flooding back with a ripply cheer
  Into every bare inlet and creek and bay.

— LOWELL

WHEN Coleridge called this

"— the leafy month of June,"

it seems to me that he struck the note of the first
summer month more distinctly than our own
Bryant, who wrote of "flowery June." June is,
above all things, "leafy," seeming chiefly to concentrate her energies on her foliage; for although
she really is not lacking in flowers, they are almost
swamped in the great green flood which has swept
silently but irresistibly across the land. At times
one loses sight of them altogether, and fancies
that a sort of reaction has set in after that

"— festival
Of breaking bud and scented breath"

which enchained our senses a few weeks since.
But the sight of a clover-field alone suffices to

dispel the thought. There is no suggestion of ex-
haustion in the close, sweet-scented, wholesome
heads which are nodding over whole acres of land.

> "South winds jostle them,
> Bumble-bees come,
> Hover, hesitate,
> Drink, and are gone,"

sings Emily Dickinson, who elsewhere calls the
clover the

> "flower that bees prefer
> And butterflies desire."

Indeed, although this is not a native blossom,
it seems to have taken a special hold on the imagination of our poets. Mr. James Whitcomb Riley
asks,

> "what is the lily and all of the rest
> Of the flowers to a man with a heart in his
> breast,
> That was dipped brimmin' full of the honey
> and dew
> Of the sweet clover-blossoms his babyhood
> knew?"

It is generally acknowledged that our sense of
smell is so intimately connected with our powers
of memory that odors serve to recall, with peculiar vividness, the particular scenes with which

they are associated. Many of us have been startled by some swiftly borne, perhaps unrecognized fragrance, which, for a brief instant, has forcibly projected us into the past; and I can imagine that a sensitively organized individual — and surely the poet is the outcome of a peculiarly sensitive and highly developed organization — might be carried back, with the strong scent of the clover-field, to the days when its breath was a sufficient joy and its limits barred out all possibility of disaster.

If we pluck from the rounded heads one tiny flower and examine it with a magnifying-glass we see that it has somewhat the butterfly shape of its kinsman, the sweet-pea of the garden. We remember that as children we followed the bee's example and sucked from its slender tube the nectar; and we conclude that the combined presence of irregularity of form, nectar, vivid coloring, and fragrance indicates a need of insect visitors for the exchange of pollen and consequent setting of seed, as Nature never expends so much effort without some clear end in view.

As an instance of the strange "web of complex relations," to quote Darwin, which binds together the various forms of life, I recall a statement, which created some amusement at a meeting of the English Royal Agricultural Society, to the effect that the growth of pink clover depended largely on the proximity of old women. The speaker argued that old women kept cats; cats killed mice; mice were prone to destroy the nests of the bumble-bees, which alone were fitted, owing to the length of their probosces, to fertilize the blossoms of the clover. Consequently, a good supply of clover depended on an abundance of old women.

The little yellow hop-clover has just begun to make its appearance in the sandy fields and along the road-sides. Although it is very common, and in spite of its general resemblance, both in leaf and flower, to the other clovers, it seems to be recognized but seldom. I have known people to gather it with unction and send it to some distant botanical friend as a rarity.

One morning last fall I found a quantity of blood-red clover-heads by the road-side. As I was gathering a few — never before having seen this species, I was confident — a woman came out from the neighboring farm-house to tell me that her husband had planted his clover-seed, as usual, the previous spring, and had been much amazed at the appearance of this flaming crop. She was eager to know if I could tell her what sort of clover it was that yielded these unusual blossoms.

A careful search through my "Gray" left me quite in the dark. Every plant-lover knows the sense of defeat that comes with the acknowledgement that you cannot place a flower, and will sympathize with the satisfaction which I experienced a few days later when, while reading in one of Mr. Burroughs's books an account of a country walk in England, I found a description of *Trifolium incarnatum,* a clover common on the other side, but comparatively recently known here, that exactly tallied with the appearance of the stranger which by some chance had found its way to the dooryard of the Connecticut farmer.

It is in the June grass that the buttercups and daisies open their eyes and take their first look at the new year. Blue-flags still lift their stately heads along the water-courses, and the blossoms of the blue-eyed grass are now so large and abundant that they seem to float like a flood of color on the tops of the long grasses. In the wet meadows, at least, the blues now predominate, rather than the yellows. The only yellow flower that seems to be abundant among the flags and blue-eyes is a day-blooming species of the evening primrose, with delicate, four-petalled flowers scattered about the upper part of the slender stems.

It is Richard Jeffries who finds fault with the artists for the profuseness with which they scattered flowers upon their canvases; but, for myself, I recall no painted meadow more thickly strewn with blossoms than the actual one which stretches before me. It seems to me that the fault to-day lies more in the quality of the painting than in the quantity of the flowers.

It is in the face of modern tradition that one wishes to see these indicated with some fidelity and tenderness; yet I cannot but feel that the old Italians — Fra Angelico, for example — caught better the spirit of the fields of Paradise when they starred them with separate, gem-like flowers, than do our modern men that of our own meadows, which they dash with reckless splashes of color, expecting the leafless, stemless blotches to do duty for the most exquisitely tinted and delicately modelled of Nature's products. And I think that one recalls more vividly in the galleries of Florence than in those of Fifty-seventh Street the near effect of the flower-spangled fields which border our Hudson.

A flower of the June fields somewhat infrequent in my experience is the painted cup. This plant owes its effectiveness, not to the blossoms, which, pale yellow in color, are rather small and inconspicuous, but to the scarlet leaves by which they are surrounded. It is one of the plants which love to grow in masses. The sensation on seeing for the first time a sunlit meadow patched with these intensely colored leaves is not soon forgotten. I always associate the painted cup with the song of the bobolink. The first time I ever met with it, the sweet morning air was alive with the

BUNCHBERRY
Cornus canadensis

happy tinkle of these birds. Their black and white coats flashed in the sunshine and hovered above or disappeared beneath the glistening grasses and gay flowers of the surrounding meadow.

In the woods of June no family is more consciously or conspicuously represented than the heaths. The small, bell-like waxen blossoms, white, pink, or actually red, of the various blueberries and huckleberries appear early in the month. In the mountains and along the New England coast we find in flower at this time a singularly attractive little plant, the mountain-cranberry. Its blossom resembles those of the blueberry group more closely than it does the flowers of the other cranberries, being bell-shaped and wax-like. It is a creeping plant and its rose-colored blossoms, growing in close clusters, nestle among the dark, shining evergreen leaves which carpet the rocky ledges near the sea or cover daintily the stones which rise up in the wood-path. It seems to me a much more perfect and picturesque plant than its relative, the trailing arbutus, but its flowers lack the rare fragrance of the latter.

The other cranberries, the small and the large, blossom later in the month, lasting sometimes well into July. Their pale-pink flowers nod from erect, thread-like stems among the slender grasses and delicate, moisture-loving plants of the peat bogs.

The reflexed petals and protruding connivent stamens of these blossoms suggest somewhat the
shooting-star of our western woods as well as its
larger kinsman, the European cyclamen. The
leaves of both species are small and evergreen,
somewhat similar to those of the mountain-cranberry.

A singularly attractive little plant belonging to
this heath tribe is the one-flowered pyrola. Its actual name, *Moneses grandiflora,* is more suggestive
of its peculiar charm. Not only is the white, waxen
flower that droops from the tip of a slender stem
strikingly large in proportion to the height of the
plant, which does not exceed, if it reaches, three
or four inches, and to the size of the rounded
leaves, which are clustered just above the ground,
but its dainty grace warrants the enthusiasm indicated by the generic name, which signifies "single delight." Then, too, the plant's intrinsic charm
is not lessened by its choice of surroundings. In
the dense shade of the evergreen forest, where we
hardly expect to find any plants in flower, little
companies of these pure blossoms nod above the
red-brown, leaf-strewn floor.

Nearly related to *Moneses* are the actual py-
rolas, lily-of-the-valley–like plants, which we find
hanging out their pretty, waxen bells along the
shaded road-side, as well as in the deeper woods.
The two most attractive members of the group,

at least in my experience, are the familiar shin-leaf, and the round-leaved species, the latter easily recognized by its leathery, shining foliage. In these two species the long, curved pistil which protrudes from the flowers easily distinguishes them from their cousin the pipsissewa. This latter plant we can recognize by means of the violet-colored anthers of its fragrant flowers, and by its glossy, evergreen leaves.

No other heaths do so much for the general reputation of the family as the laurels and rhododendrons. The mountain-laurel reaches perfection during the latter half of June. Where it grows, the wood-openings look like great drifts of snow, the snow of an Alpine dawn, for often in sunny places the flowers of the mountain-laurel are pure rose-color, though in the deeper woods they are white.

The thick, glossy leaves form an effective background to the dense clusters of wholesome-looking flowers. Perhaps the firm, fluted, pink-tinged buds are even prettier than the blossoms. Pick a freshly opened cluster and observe that each of the ten little bags of pollen is caught in a separate depression of the wheel-shaped corolla. Brush the flower, lightly but quickly, with your finger or a twig, and you see that the bags are dislodged by the jar with such force that your finger is thickly dusted with pollen, and you understand how the visiting bee unconsciously transmits the precious grains from flower to flower.

Perhaps the wax-like, delicately spotted flowers of the rhododendron are even handsomer than those of the laurel, but in our northern latitude they are far less abundant and much less luxuriant in their manner of growth.

Often in company with the mountain-laurel and the rhododendron, but commonly in less exclusive haunts, we find the sheep-laurel or lambkill, a somewhat straggling little shrub with pale, narrowly oblong leaves and clusters of pink or reddish blossoms. They are fresh, vigorous-looking flowers, specially effective when massed against the gray rocks of the seashore, among clumps of bay-berry and wild-rose bushes.

An interesting flower, due in early June, is the arethusa, one of the orchid family. Its usual home is a cranberry-swamp, and the ones I have had the good-fortune to find were growing near groups of young larches, for whose companionship I believe they are known to have a special liking. The blossom has been described as "crystalline purple." It crowns a slender stalk which bears below a single grass-like leaf. The narrow sepals and petals arch above the petal-like columns. The dilated lip is yellow-bearded. The flower has a startled, alert look, as though it were pricking its delicate ears in alarm at some rude intrusion. That I have not detected the fragrance which is said to belong to the arethusa may be owing only to my tardiness, for I have never found her till some time after her legitimate blossoming season. The remoteness of her haunts has put her usually out of my reach, and she still remains an incentive to greater punctuality next year, and a stimulant to the eagerness aroused by each approaching spring.

Another of the many fascinating inhabitants of the cranberry-swamps is the pitcher-plant. In Maine I found it in great quantities budding and in full bloom on June 14th of this year, which means that farther south it was due one or two weeks earlier. At this time all the flowers were hanging their heads, showing only the lower surfaces of their sepals, "a shiny leather-red or brown-red" in color, "looking as if newly varnished, very rich and pleasant to the eye," writes Thoreau. When examined more closely, the inside of the sepals are seen to be green. The petals are red and extremely delicate in texture, suggesting "a great, dull-red rose." At this early stage of the plant's development the only mature leaves seem to be those left over from the previous year, looking rusty and worn outside, but perfectly water-tight, filled to the brim with water in which float the bodies of many drowned insects.

Although it may be found during the first part of July, to this month of June belongs, I think, the most regal of our orchids, the showy lady's-slipper. Its favorite home is a somewhat shaded peat-bog. Here the great, leafy-stemmed plants, with their lovely pink and white shell-like flowers, seem to reach their fullest development. There is something almost tropical in their lavish, luxuriant beauty. Fortunately their chosen haunts are usually somewhat inaccessible, so, despite the great bunches which are exhibited for sale by energetic farmers' boys at New England inns and country houses, there is still reason to hope that they will not be completely exterminated.

One of the smallest and loveliest of the wood-loving plants of June is the twin-flower, *Linnaea borealis,* the tiny

"monument of the man of flowers."

Often as I stroll along the wood-path, my body only under the trees, perhaps, my thoughts wandering elsewhere, I am recalled to myself by a fresh, penetrating odor, and I see the carpet of small, rounded leaves and thread-like forking stems which are hung with the pink-veined sister-blossoms. The twin-flower shares the faculty possessed by *Moneses* of choosing attractive surroundings. It likes to cover the mossy banks of shaded streams and to fill the hollows formed by

the great roots of the forest trees. The most se-
questered nooks we chance upon in our explorations of the northern woods in June are likely to
be adorned by the pink bells of the *Linnaea*.

Another wood-plant, a little less fastidious,
perhaps, in its choice of locality, is the Indian
cucumber-root, or *Medeola*. This is rather an
unusual-looking plant, delicate and graceful, with
small green or yellowish, lily-like flowers which
droop from the summit of a slender stem. Directly beneath the flower-cluster grows a whorl of
ovate, pointed leaves; still farther down, the stem
is again encircled by another whorl consisting of
more and larger leaves. The plant is less effective
now than later in the summer, when its erect, purple berries and gayly painted leaves are sure to
attract the eye. I have never tasted the tuberous
root, which is said to have a cucumber-like flavor
and to have been used as food by the Indians.

Even in midwinter we can go to the woods,
and, brushing away the snow from about the roots
of some old tree, find the shining, white-veined
leaves and coral-like berries of the partridge-vine.
But this is the season when we should make a
special pilgrimage to some dim retreat which is
pervaded with the fragrance of its lovely white or
pinkish twin blossoms.

Among fallen, moss-grown tree-trunks we find
the clover-like leaflets and pink-veined flowers of

the true wood-sorrel. These flowers are strikingly large in proportion to the rest of the plant. The pale green foliage is singularly fresh and delicate. One is not surprised to learn that it was a favorite plant of the old Italian painters, and that its dainty symmetry appealed especially to Fra Angelico.

So frequent and enchanting are the revelations which await us these days that, to the man or woman with unburdened mind and enlightened vision, a country ramble is one of the most perfect of pleasures. Then there are days when the odor-laden winds seem to have some narcotic power, lulling to inertia all energy and ambition; days when the drowsily witnessed voyage of a butter-fly, or the half-heard song of a wood-thrush, or even the dreamy consciousness of the rhythmical development of life about us — the measured succession of bud, flower, and fruit — seems a sufficient end in itself.

It is easier to resist this influence if we keep to the road. Once we are led away by some winding pretence of a path, each leafy curve of which is more enticing than the last, we are apt to yield ourselves to the simple charm of being. But on the road we are more practical, more self-conscious. We cease entirely to be self-conscious only when there is no chance of human interruption. On the road a farm-wagon may overtake us at any moment, and we feel that, to the bovine mind, even the foolish occupation of picking flowers seems more intelligent than the abandonment of one's self to joy in the blue of the sky or in the breath of summer.

Among the shrubs which flower in June, the viburnums and the dogwoods are noticeable. The somewhat flat flower-clusters of the viburnums are made up of small, white, five-lobed blossoms, the little flowers of the superficially similar dogwoods consisting of four petals. The leaves of most of the viburnums are more or less conspicuously toothed, while those of the dogwoods are entire. The withe-rod, *V. cassinoides,* a shrub which I find growing abundantly along the coast and in the woods of northern New England, is an exception to this rule, its thick, smooth, ovate or oblong leaves being toothed only very little or not at all.

Along grassy lanes the wild-grape swings its graceful festoons. The air is heavy with the sweet breath of its greenish flowers. Near by twist the prickly stems, shining ornamental leaves, and greenish blossoms of the cat-brier. The carrion-vine, too, sends forth its delicate young shoots, but the foul odor of its dull, clustered blossoms, which has attracted all the carrion-liking flies in the neighborhood, drives us hurriedly from its vicinity.

Over the rocks and about the trunks and close branches of slim cedars twine the stout stems and glossy leaves of the poison-ivy. If we are wise, we tarry here no longer than by the carrion-vine, for the small white flowers, now fully open, are said to give forth peculiarly poisonous emanations.

Flat rosettes of purple-veined leaves and tall clusters of dandelion-like flower-heads abound by the dusty highway. The striped leaves suggested the markings of the rattlesnake to some imaginative mind, and so the plant has been dubbed "rattlesnake weed," and the superstitious have used it as a cure for the bites of the rattlesnake. Narrow leaves and pretty, spotted flowers on hair-like stalks grow in many circles about the slender stems of the yellow loosestrife.

The blackberry vines wreathe everything within reach with their graceful branches and large, delicate flowers. The slender, light-blue clusters of the larger skull-cap are beginning to be noticeable. Through the grasses glistens the wet scarlet of wild-strawberries. In the thicket are shrubs, whose green buds are still too firmly closed for us to guess their names, unless we chance to recognize their leaves. There is always something to look forward to — something to come back for — even along the road-side.

June divides with May the honors of the song and nesting season. If we admit that June has fewer nests, we are inclined to claim for her more songs. Almost any early morning in June the neighborhood of a garden, orchard, or field will supply us with a bird concert of great beauty and variety. Of course, the quality of the individual singers is largely governed by the latitude. In the neighborhood of Albany, for example, besides those birds already mentioned, I expect to hear the warbling of yellow-throated vireos, of the grosbeak, scarlet tanager, indigo-bird, gold-finch, and redstart, of the black-throated green, yellow, and other warblers. In the mountains and farther north (I am thinking especially of the Maine coast) two of the thrushes, the olive-backed and the hermit, are noticeable. The song of the olive-backed thrush varies greatly. At times it is really melodious, but it has a throaty quality which de-tracts from its charm. It lacks the purity and sweetness so striking in the songs of the wood and hermit thrushes. It is longer, less interrupted, and less definite in its phrasing than these other songs. Indeed, it hardly seems to me a song at all; more actually a fairly melodious outburst of emo-tion. The bird is usually a trifle smaller than the wood-thrush and equally larger than the hermit. Its olive-brown head, bill, and tail, and its unspotted throat help to identify it.

The song of the hermit-thrush is a marvel of sweetness and spirituality, with the hymn-like quality so noticeable in that of the wood-thrush. But it is much shorter, and less of an actual song than one would suppose from the usual descriptions. Commonly I hear it repeated twice with a very brief interval of time, in different keys, the second higher than the first. After a longer interval the repetition takes place again, and continues indefinitely. Both birds belong to the deeper woods, their songs reaching one from some shadowy seclusion where they can be traced with difficulty.

One of the attractive possibilities of a wood-walk in June is the flushing of a covey of partridges. The thrill of excitement as the whirr of their wings strikes our ears is enhanced by the probable dash of the mother-bird across our path, with trailing wing and every appearance of serious injury, in the effort, usually successful, to distract our attention from the young chicks, which scurry away in another direction. The brown and white markings of these birds blend so perfectly with the leaf-strewn, sun-flecked ground, and with the brown twigs and tree-trunks, that were it not for their panic we would hardly discover their proximity.

But the June woods are full of possibilities in every direction. A song till now unheard, a new nest, a rare flower, are only a few of the many rewards we may hope to win if we are patient and loving seekers.

7

A
LONG ISLAND
MEADOW

O unestranged birds and bees!
O face of nature always true!

— LOWELL

Its entrance is barred by lichen-covered rails. Close by, a tall willow stands sentinel. The fence beyond is almost hidden by a thicket of wild-roses and elder-bushes. Against the bars crowds a host of "weeds" — burdock, wild-carrot, elecampane, and sorrel. But one feels that these are interlopers and have little in common with the more retiring inhabitants of the meadow which lies fresh and glistening in the sunlight, swaying with every breath of wind, darkening with each cloud that floats overhead, untracked and tempting. We need only to glance at such a meadow as this — and there are hundreds like it along our coast — to guess that it will be many days before its treasures are even half discovered. It is a miniature world, with grassy uplands and quaking bogs, with stretches of water and wooded

islands. Each part of this little world has its individual secrets to reveal, its own wealth of plant
and animal life.

Beyond the invading weeds is a thick growth
of cinnamon-ferns which do not seem happy in
their surroundings, a fact accounted for when we
notice that here the meadow is a dry marsh, not
affording the ferns sufficient nourishment for
their full development. They hold themselves
rigid and erect, and are quite without the grace
and stateliness for which usually they are conspicuous. The woolly-stemmed, cinnamon-colored
fruit-clusters which spring from the centre of the
plant are now withered and either cling to the
stalks of the green fronds or lie upon the ground.

Scattered among the cinnamon-ferns are clusters of the royal fern, a kinsman that appears
equally ill at ease. Its stature is stunted and its
uncompromising air fails to suggest the bearing
which won for it the title of royal fern.

The interrupted fern, the other member of
what is, perhaps, our most distinguished group of
native ferns, the osmundas, grows back against
the fence. It seems somewhat less affected by its
environment, although the erect fronds which
fruit half way up the midrib, set, as it were, in a
vase formed by the shorter, outward-curving,
sterile fronds, are less noticeable for their height
than when found under conditions more to their
liking.

CALYPSO

Calypso bulbosa

High above these dwarfed representatives of a royal family shoot the tall white wands of the colic-root. At the first glance, one unfamiliar with this plant might confuse its long clusters with the twisted spikes of the ladies' tresses. A closer examination would reveal no likeness between the flower of the orchid and the six-lobed blossom of the colic-root, with its six stamens, its three-cleft pistil, and its look of being dusted with white meal. Then, too, the flat rosette of lance-shaped leaves from which springs the white wand of flowers, is peculiar to this plant.

Over the moss which carpets this ferny upland the running swamp-blackberry trails its reddish stems, with their smooth, thick leaves and its berries still green. Here and there we find its white blossom. It is a decorative plant and one is tempted to carry home certain long, lithe strands which bear at the same time flowers and fruit.

Now the land slopes downward. The grasses and sedges wear that rich green which warns us to look out for a swamp. It is not easy to be cautious, for suddenly we get a glimpse of some vivid purplish-pink flowers which grow in singularly airy clusters on a slender stem. An orchid is always a "find," and we recognize with delight one of our most radiant orchids, the grass-pink or calopogon, which is fairly illuminating this part of the meadow with its countless blossoms.

The grass-pink differs from other members of

its family in that the lip, with its beard of white, yellow, and purple hairs, stands on the upper instead of on the lower side of the flower. This peculiarity it owes to the fact that its ovary has not the twist habitual to orchids. Despite the difference of position in that part of the flower which is specially designed to attract insects, the grass-pink is as well fitted as its sisters to secure cross-fertilization, as a careful study of its internal structure will prove.

Here the meadow becomes a bog. High rubber boots are necessary as a protection from the water and black mud in which they sink so deep that it is a question as to how long they will be of any service. The grasses grow tall and rank and gleaming. Pools of black water alternate with little islands where the marsh shield-fern holds itself well out of the wet, its segments growing high up on the stem as though trying to keep dry under discouraging conditions. If you pick one of its delicate fronds (if you happen to be an observer of ferns) you are struck with its resemblance to another fern which abounds along the road-side, but which differs from this in that its lowest segments grow gradually very much shorter, so that its frond really tapers both ways from the middle, while here the tapering at the lower part of the frond is very slight. Then, too, you observe that in this fern the stalk is usually longer than the rest of the frond, and that in certain cases the segments have a curled-over appearance, partially accounted for when you discover that these curled-over ferns bear on their backs the little round fruit-dots which are not found on the other flatter fronds. Once you are familiar with these distinguishing traits of the marsh shield-fern, you are not likely to confuse it with its equally ubiquitous kinsman, the New York shield-fern.

In and out among the ferns creep the cranberry-vines. An occasional rose-pink, four-cleft blossom still nods from an erect, leafy stem, although everywhere hang the green berries, some of them already with sunburned cheeks.

Here, too, we find that rarely lovely orchid, the adder's mouth. The plant itself is smaller than that of the grass-pink, but the rose-colored, fragrant flower which usually nods alone from the summit of the stem is quite as large as are the blossoms of its neighbor.

Far beneath the silvery pennons of the cotton-grass, down in the black mud, perhaps in the water itself, grows a curious, pretty little plant, the round-leaved sundew, with its rosette of glistening, red-haired leaves and its unfolding crosier of flower-buds, which open one at a time, and then only in the sunlight, displaying a small, white, five-petalled blossom.

The black bog-land is fairly carpeted with this

plant, which gives a jewelled look to the under-world of the meadow. It is but slightly fastened in the moist earth, and it is worth our while to up-root it and make a study of its delicately spangled leaves.

These are nearly round, narrowing somewhat abruptly into the flat stems. Each leaf bears a mul-titude of small red hairs, as many at times as two hundred to a leaf. These hairs are tipped with what seem to be tiny dew-drops, but which are in reality particles of a sticky fluid exuded by the hairs for the purpose of capturing insects.

The young leaves are rolled in the bud, or par-tially unrolled after the fashion of young fern fronds. Others are fully open, each hair sparkling with its jewelled tip. Still others look withered, and black particles seem to be held in the depres-sion of the leaf-blade.

One must be familiar with the habits of the sundew to know that these black particles are the remains of the bodies of insects which have been attracted to the leaf by the apparent presence of drops of nectar. In these drops their legs are first caught; then the red hairs bend slowly over and imprison still more helplessly the little body, which is soon lifeless. A digestive fluid is now ex-uded from the hairs, and the flesh and blood are absorbed by the plant, which leaves undigested only the bony portions that form the particles left upon the surface of the leaf. Two days are said to be sufficient for the total absorption of the digestible parts of the body of a very small insect. After this absorption is accomplished, the leaf and the hairs slowly recover their former position. Within a day or two, fresh drops of the deceptive fluid are exuded, and the murderous work begins anew. One leaf may capture many prisoners. Ants, flies, beetles, and even butterflies are numbered among the victims of this little plant.

Of the three species of sundew native to this part of the country, I find two here, the round-leaved and the oblong-leaved, the latter noticeable from its habit of raising itself upon its root, so as not to be submerged when growing in the water.

Springing directly out of the black pools which the sundews border is a slender, usually leafless stem, bearing a yellow flower with a projecting, helmet-shaped lip. In the water at the base of the stem float little, awl-shaped leaves, fastened to which are a number of tiny sacs or bladders. This is the bladderwort, a plant which would naturally find the neighborhood of the sundew congenial, as it is another of the insect-eating group. Its bladders are so small as to give no hint of the death-traps that they are, but a careful look into their interiors will discover the remains of insects lured to their destruction as cleverly and as surely as are the victims of the sundew. Each bladder is furnished with a door which opens inward. It is supposed that insects when pursued by enemies seek its shelter, rushing into involuntary imprisonment, as the door by which they entered will not open outward. They die from starvation or suffocation, and specially adapted cells of the bladder absorb the particles of their decomposed bodies.

Close to the bladderwort, where the pools widen into miniature lakes, a multitude of slender stems tipped with white knobs rise from the water. These white-knobbed stems belong to the seven-angled pipewort, a curious little plant that bears its minute blossoms closely clustered in the knobs which first attracted our attention. Its thread-like leaves, tufted at the base of the stem, are partly out of sight under the water.

All about us are mossy hummocks where cranberry and swamp-blackberry vines interlace their spreading strands; where the marsh shield-fern and the sensitive fern contend for standing-room; where the aromatic leaves of the bayberry bask in the sunshine, and the dull spikes of the ragged-fringed orchis erect themselves with inconspicuous grace, their small flowers not impressing the eye, although already the individual, deeply fringed blossoms deserve more than passing notice.

Wandering among these chosen footholds of

the ragged-fringed orchis is a narrow, sluggish stream, almost hidden from sight by clumps of royal fern and by thickets of wild-roses and aza-leas. Here the three-toothed orchis is in bud. At first it seems likely that this is another species, as the botanists assign *Habenaria tridentata* to "wet woods," but later a careful analysis of a full-blown blossom confirms me in my first conjecture. The botanical description, "stem, slender; leaf, single, oblong; flowers, greenish or whitish, very small; lip, wedge-oblong, truncate, and with three short teeth at apex, the slender and slightly club-shaped spur curved upward, longer than the ovary; root, of few fleshy fibres," seems to apply satisfactorily to this little plant, with a possible exception in the case of the "very small" flowers, the blossoms which make up these spikes being small, but not exceptionally so.

We have crossed the meadow and reached a tangled thicket of alder and bayberry bushes, of wild-roses, with a few delicate blossoms still open to the bees and sunshine, of white swamp honey-suckle, even yet bearing some fragrant clusters, and of *Clethra*, whose green, budding spikes hold fast their treasure of beauty and fragrance. Out of sight a cat-bird is mewing discordantly, and on some lower twigs a Maryland yellow-throat, with bright yellow body and black cheeks, hops busily about. A swallow flies close above our heads, through the sweet, sunny air. Across the thicket comes the ever-recurrent sighing of the sea.

Now the land rises and we are on *terra firma* once more. Here the pasture-thistles hold up their superb purple flower-heads, and farther on we see reddish patches that prove to be the meadow-beauty, sometimes called Kentucky grass. The flower is an attractive one, noticeable from its large rounded red-purple petals, and from its eight protruding stamens, each of which is tipped with a long curved yellow anther.

In this corner of the meadow we find tall brakes and light-green sensitive ferns in abundance. If we push aside the sterile fronds of the latter, the fruit-clusters of this year and the brown empty pods of those of last year are soon discovered, although these clusters here, as nearly always, are so hidden from sight as to be a novelty to most people.

I think it is Mr. Bradford Torrey who says that when he goes to walk as a botanist his ornithological senses are sealed. He is alive only to plants. He neither sees nor hears the birds. And, *vice versa,* when he goes bird-hunting, the green growing things about have no definite existence for him.

This tendency is natural enough and may easily be carried even to greater lengths. When on the lookout for flowers, it may chance that not only

PINK AZALEA
Rhododendron nudiflorum

some rare bird or brilliant butterfly escapes our notice, but that such plants as do not flower, or as do not bear what we are accustomed to look upon as flowers, fail utterly to arrest our attention.

Perhaps the reason for this is that we are more apt to notice the things about which we have some knowledge, and in this busy world it is a difficult matter to know even a little about many different things. So in our walks abroad we concentrate our attention upon our own especial hobby, be this flowers or ferns, birds or butterflies.

But in such a spot as this, to one who has confined himself to a single hobby, there comes a sense of limitation, of painful inadequacy, which spurs him to the resolve to strive after broader knowledge, or, for it is the same thing, broader enjoyment. At least some such experience as this has been mine during the hours I have lately passed in this meadow. The flowers, nearly all of them, are old friends. The ferns, too, are not strangers. But as to the names and habits of these beautiful, grass-like, sedge-like, rush-like things that wave and float and sway above the flowers, above the ferns, I was almost entirely at sea. For years I had meant to make a study of the grasses and sedges, but the empty days they were designed to fill slipped farther and farther into the future, and here I was among a host of lovely, tantalizing creatures who were quite nameless. I hurried home from my first visit to the meadow with the determination to learn from some book at least the names of the strangers. With the happy confidence of ignorance, I felt assured that by another day I should feel more at home among them.

But my confidence was premature. The flower-lover who seeks to know as well as to love, finds himself somewhat daunted on his first introduction to "coherent" calyxes, "superior" ovaries, "deciduous" sepals, and "parietal" placentae. But what are these to "imbricated two-ranked glumes," with their "palets" and "lodicules," their "caryopses" and "ligules"? It is bad enough to have the glumes "imbricated," but when they become "excurrent" or "chartaceous" or "ventricose-scarious-margined" at the same time; when they are so small as to be almost invisible, and when the pygmy-like proportions of "palets" render them absolutely intangible, then the seeker after superficial knowledge, by means of which he hopes to satisfy himself and to astonish his neighbors, is reduced to despair.

At last, however, I did grasp the fact that grasses are "usually" hollow-stemmed save at the joints, and that their sheathing leaves are "split or open on the side opposite the blade" (what the "hypogynous" flowers "usually" were about, I refused even to attempt to discover), and that sedges had "mostly" (but, oh, the exceptions in science) "solid stems and closed sheaths" (the habits of their "spiked, chiefly three-androus flowers" I also left religiously alone); and armed with this double piece of information, back I went to the meadow.

That sunny, breezy morning almost the first objects to catch my eye were certain long-stemmed creatures tip-toeing on a hummock near the plantation of cinnamon-ferns, with ribbon-like leaves apparently knotted about their necks and floating on the wind. "A sedge, without doubt," I thought, cutting reluctantly one of the vigorous stems. But an eager look showed that this was hollow, and another glance seemed to prove that it was *not* an exception. It could not be a grass, as its "sheathing leaves" were neither "split nor open on the side opposite the blade." Yet it looked *so* easy.

When persuaded that the lovely, rollicking thing was neither grass nor sedge, I found that the family description of rushes left the inside of *their* stems to the imagination, and so far as stems were concerned (and I began to rejoice in my primitive method of classification) it seemed to me that I was free to call it a rush. So I christened it "Moorland Princess" and felt almost (but I will frankly admit not quite) as happy as when I learned later that despite the misleading hollowness of its stem, my Moorland Princess was nevertheless a sedge and was legally entitled to the not altogether euphonious name of *Scirpus cyperinus.*

On the next hunt I had better luck. Out of the black water where the sundews and bladderworts had laid their clever little traps, grows a wilderness of triangular, grass-like leaves (as they seemed to me), from each of which, near its nodding summit, protrudes a bunch of brown knobs. It was easy to see that what looked like the plant's leaf was its stem or "culm"; that this was "solid," as the culm of a sedge should be, and "sharply triangular," as the particular sedge called "chairmaker's rush" must be, for after much reading of description and consultation of the plates in the back of Gray's manual, and in Dr. Britton's new, delightful book, which gives us pictures of everything, the "chairmaker's rush" (although a sedge) I decided this abundant and effective plant to be.

Next I discovered the identity of the "smooth marsh grass," a tall, graceful creature with ribbon-like leaves, and alternate branching spikes of flowers, which let out a fringe of tremulous purple stamens. Another abundant plant with round stems and little brown flower-clusters I placed without difficulty among the rushes, and identified as the "common bog rush."

Other plants belonging to one or another of these three groups, grasses, sedges, and rushes, either by my own efforts or with the help of wiser friends, I succeeded later in placing as "panic grass," "dropseed," "bog bulrush," "red-rooted Cyperus," "twig-rush," etc., while still others I pressed and laid aside for future identification, trying to take comfort in the thought that even the infinitely patient Darwin found himself baffled by the grasses.

I think one seldom realizes more keenly the swift flight of summer than when watching the changes which take place in some one clearly de-fined spot such as this meadow. It seemed as though I had only begun to revel in the grace of the grass-pinks and adder's mouths, when a few days of storm intervened, and, on my next visit, grass-pinks and adder's mouths had vanished, with the exception of here and there some belated and reluctant blossom. From the mossy hum-mocks the ragged-fringed orchis had almost dis-appeared. Deep down among the grasses the three-toothed orchis had blossomed and begun to wither. The little flower-clusters of the sundew had gone to seed, and only here and there could be found a solitary yellow blossom of the blad-derwort. Cranberries and blackberries had deep-ened in color, wild-roses and elder-blossoms had given place to hips and berries.

But above the cinnamon-ferns glowed spots of orange-red. From stately stems set round with slender leaves nodded the burning blossoms of the Turk's-cap lily, its long recurved sepals spotted with red-brown, its stamens tipped with pollen-laden anthers which trembled with every breath of wind. In all the neighborhood I have not found the wood or meadow lily, but their places are amply filled by these voluptuous-looking creatures.

The under-world among the sedges, which the week before was radiant with bright-flowered orchids, is now enlivened by the red stems, changing leaves, and dainty flesh-colored flowers of the marsh St. Johnswort. This little plant is already taking on the burning colors of the fall, giving us a foretaste of October.

Near the stream the spotted cowbane sends up its streaked stems and spreads the white irregular flower-clusters that pronounce it akin to the wild-carrot. On its very borders the pink spires of the steeple-bush rise far above their oblong leaves, whose woolly lining protects them from the heavy moisture which rises at nightfall from the surrounding marsh.

Perhaps the most noticeable of all the changes in the meadow is that which has taken place on almost every hummock, along the borders of the stream and especially in the thicket. Everywhere are the sharply toothed, oblong, alder-like leaves and erect white flower-clusters of the *Clethra*. The fragrance of these wax-like flowers adds a new charm and freshness to the August morning.

Another conspicuous arrival in the meadow is the great burnet. This is a tall plant with leaflets somewhat like those of the rose, and long-stalked spikes of feathery white flowers, the lower ones opening first, leaving the upper part of the spike in bud. These blossoms owe their feathery appearance to the four long white stamens of which each blossom seems chiefly to consist, the four petal-like lobes of the calyx having fallen and the pistil being inconspicuous.

The brilliant coloring which is a feature of this midsummer meadow is intensified by the insect life which it sustains. Butterflies, especially, seem to abound. They float over the nodding grasses or poise quivering above a nectar-laden blossom or rest on some leafy plant, the dull undersides of their folded wings blending with their surroundings and diminishing the likelihood of attacks from their enemies.

Not only is a butterfly endowed with unusual beauty, but its life-history is full of charm. Then, too, the very names of butterflies (unlike those of birds and plants, of many of which "Wilson's thrush" and "Clayton's fern" form fair samples) breathe romance. Who would not yield to the spell of the Wanderer, the Brown Elfin, the Little Wood Satyr, and the Dreamy Dusky-wing? Or who could resist the charm of the Painted Lady, the Silver-spotted Hesperid, the Tawny Emperor, or the Red Admiral?

In the meadow, perhaps, the monarch or milkweed butterfly is one of the most omnipresent. Indeed, this is probably the best-known butterfly in the United States, as its broad, orange-red, black-bordered wings carry it many hundreds of miles and make it conspicuous everywhere.

In addition to being the most widely distributed, it is one of the most interesting of our butterflies. Its career is an amazing one. How so fragile a creature can endure the fatigue and resist the storm and stress incidental to a journey of thousands of miles, such as it is believed to take when migrating to southern lands, and how such a "shining mark" escapes destruction from its enemies, it is difficult to understand. That this annual migration does take place seems fairly well established. The butterfly is known to have marvellous powers of flight, and along the coast in the fall it has frequently been seen assembling in flocks numbering hundreds of thousands, changing the color of the trees on which it alights for the night.

Its great weapon against its enemies, the birds, is the rank odor exhaled from its entire body, as

COTTON-GRASS
Eriophorum virginicum and *E. gracile*

well as a specially nauseous smell produced by the males at will by means of a bunch of hairs protruding from either side of the abdomen.

This safeguard is supposed to be the cause of what is called the "unconscious mimicry" of another tribe of butterflies which wear the same livery of orange and black. It is, perhaps, hardly necessary to say that this so-called "mimicry" is believed to be the result of long periods of time during which only those members of the *Basilarchia* that bore some resemblance to the monarch butterfly contrived to live long enough to leave descendants; as a consequence, from generation to generation the likeness between the two tribes increased, till at last the *Basilarchia* so successfully counterfeited the appearance of the milkweed butterfly that, while still without its weapons of defence, it secured almost the same immunity from its enemies.

The scent perception of butterflies is astonishingly keen. Their vision has been proved to be very imperfect, according to our ideas, and it is believed that they are guided to the plants upon which they wish to lay their eggs, and from which they hope to gather food, by the sense of smell, rather than by that of sight. It is claimed that in certain tribes a female butterfly, emerging from her cocoon quite out of sight and several miles away (in a city, for instance) from any of her tribe is speedily visited by her kinsmen who have been guided hither by the sense of smell alone.

Clinging to a leaf or a blade of grass, occasionally we see the caterpillar of the milkweed butterfly, its plump body banded with yellow, black, and white. These caterpillars come from eggs deposited by the butterfly upon the upper surface of the new leaves of the family food-plant (usually a milkweed). In about four days the caterpillar hatches, and spends the next two or three weeks, while attaining its size, upon the food-plant. During this period it moults its skin four times. When the time comes for the change to chrysalis, it usually leaves the food-plant and seeks some safe and steady spot, where it hangs from nine to fifteen days, when the butterfly emerges.

In and out among the butterflies flashes the darning-needle, its blue gleam recalling those childish days when we fearfully hid our ears lest they be darned together. Big green grasshoppers cling to the leaves and grass-blades, whose exact color they often seem to reproduce, another case of the mimicry which brings security. Under the grasses crawls the great black, furry spider whose bite, tradition tells us, is death, and seeming to me more like the incarnation of the spirit of evil than any other thing I know, save a black snake. In the centre of its beautiful upright web close by watches another huge, poisonous-looking creature with black body, spotted and banded with light yellow.

Upon the foot-path along the fence lies the empty shell of a turtle. Farther on the skin of a snake is drying in the sun. At times I am more grateful for the protection which my rubber-boots afford me from furry spiders and other crawling, creeping things which I picture in the black slime below the sedges than from the mud in which I sink almost knee-deep.

I wonder if education could secure one against the vague unreasoning horror with which certain grewsome-looking creatures always inspire one. This horror does not arise altogether from fear of any actual physical harm. One fears a ferocious bull, yet it is doubtful if the thought of the great beast fills him with the sort of shrinking terror which is aroused by the mere memory of other comparatively harmless creatures. Yet where actually repellent objects are concerned, I doubt if it would be possible to plant in even young and unprejudiced minds the desirable sense of kinship with all living things.

It is the last week of August. The meadow is putting on its dress of gold and purple, the red-gold of the pendants of the jewel-weed, the yellow-gold of the golden-rod, the blue-purples of the asters, the pinker shades of the sea-side gerardia, the lavender of the bell-like flower-heads of the lion's foot, and the varied purples of the blossoming grasses, now more luxuriant than ever.

The bird-voices grow daily more rare. An occasional song-sparrow makes a hoarse effort, but is less successful than are the myriad insects, the crickets, locusts, and grasshoppers. These fill the air with a droning, soothing chorus that blends with the low roar of the sea beyond the distant sand-hills.

8

MIDSUMMER

Or else perhaps I sought some meadow low,
Where deep-fringed orchids reared their feathery spires,
　Where lilies nodded by the river slow,
　And milkweeds burned in red and orange fires;
Where bright-winged blackbirds flashed like living coals,
　And reed-birds fluted from the swaying grass;
　There shared I in the laden bee's delight,
　Quivered to see the dark cloud-shadows pass
Beyond me; loved and yearned to know the souls
Of bird and bee and flower — of day and night.

IT IS INTERESTING to observe the manner in which the flowers express the dominant mood of the season. The early ones, as has been noticed already, are chilly-looking, shy, tentative; charming with the shrinking, uncertain charm of an American spring. Those of the later year are distinctly hardy, braced to meet cold winds and nipping nights; while those of midsummer — those which are abroad now — have caught the hot look of flame, or of the sun itself, or — at times — the deep blue of the sky.

Of course there are exceptions to this rule, as we shall note later; but the least observing must admit the intensity of the colors which now prevail, colors which are not, perhaps, more brilliant than the later ones, but which, it seems to me, are far more suggestive of summer. It may be argued

that this is merely a matter of association: that
if the golden-rods and asters were in the habit
of flowering in July, and if the lilies and milkweeds ordinarily postponed their appearance
till September, the former would seem to us the
ones which embodied most vividly the idea of heat
and sunlight, while the latter would typify, in
a perfectly satisfactory fashion, the colder season.

I am ready to acknowledge that we are victim-
ized sometimes by our sensitiveness to association; recalling clearly a certain childish conviction
that one could recognize Sunday by the peculiarly
golden look of its sunlight, and by the long, mysterious slant of its shadows in the orchard. This
delusion — though even yet it hardly seems
that — sprang, I suppose, partly from the fact
that only on Sunday was one obliged to refrain
from a variety of enchanting pursuits which at
other times proved so absorbing as to preclude
any great sensitiveness to the aspects of nature,
and partly also from a certain serenity in the
moral atmosphere which so linked itself with the
visible surroundings as to arouse the belief that
the lights and shadows of this one day actually
differed in character from those of the other six.
Still I cannot but think that not only is the coarse-
ness of habit common to the later flowers suggestive of a defensive attitude in view of a more or

WOOD LILY
Lilium philadelphicum

less inclement season, but that their actual colors are less indicative of the heat of summer.

Surely no autumn field sends upward a multiple reflection of the sun itself as do these meadows about us. One would suppose that the yellow rays of the omnipresent black-eyed Susan would droop beneath the fierce ones which beat upon them from above. Instead, they seem to welcome the touch of a kinsman and to gain vigor from the contact. One instantly recognizes these flowers as members of the great composite family, a tribe which is beginning to take almost undisputed possession of many of our fields; that is, in relation to the floral world, for the farmers are waging constant war upon it. They are cousins of the dandelions and daisies, of the golden-rod and asters.

The family name indicates that each flower-head is composed of a number of small flowers which are clustered so closely as to give the effect of a single blossom. In the black-eyed Susan the brown centre, the "black eye" itself, consists of a quantity of tubular-shaped blossoms, which are crowded upon a somewhat cone-shaped receptacle, hence the common name of "cone-flower." In botanical parlance, these are called "disk-flowers." They possess both stamens and pistils, while the yellow rays, which commonly are regarded as petals, are in reality flowers which are without of these important organs; only assisting in the perpetuation of the species by arresting the attention of passing insects and thus securing an exchange of pollen among the perfect disk-flowers.

In the common daisy the arrangement is different. Here the white rays are even more useful than ornamental, as they are the female flowers of the head, eventually producing seed; while the yellow disk-flowers of the centre yield the pollen. The dandelion is without any tubular blossoms. Its florets are botanically described as "strap-shaped," resembling the ray-flowers of the daisy and black-eyed Susan. In the common thistle, again, we find only tubular flowers. If the minute blossoms of the composite family were not thus grouped, probably they would be too inconspicuous to attract attention and often might fail to secure the pollen necessary to their fertilization. To quote Mr. Grant Allen, "Union is strength for the daisy as for the State."

More people would learn to take an interest in plants if they suspected the pleasurable excitement which awaits the flower-lover upon the most commonplace railway journey. A peculiar thrill of expectancy is caused by the rapidly changing environment which reveals, in swift succession, flowers of the most varied proclivities. If we leave New York on a certain road, at intervals for an hour or more the salt marshes spread their deep-hued treasures before us. Then we turn into the interior, passing through farmlands where the plants which follow in the wake of civilization line our way. Suddenly we leave these behind. Darting into the deep forest we catch glimpses of the shyer woodland beauties. Now and then we span a foaming river, on whose steep shores we may detect, with the eagerness of a sportsman, some long-sought rarity.

It is always a fresh surprise and disappointment to me to find that I can seldom reach on foot such wild and promising spots as the railway window reveals. Is it possible that the swiftly vanishing scene has been illuminated by the imagination which has been allowed the freer play from the improbability of any necessity for future readjustment? However that may be, I find that my book possesses but little charm till an aching head warns me to refrain from too constant a vigil.

Just now, from such a coign of vantage, when the unclouded sun beats upon their surfaces, certain pastures look as though afire. The grasses sway about great patches of intense orange-red, suggestive of creeping flames. This startling effect is given by the butterfly-weed, the most gorgeous member of the milkweed family. Almost equally vivid, though less flame-like, is the purple milkweed, a species which abounds also in dry places, with deep pink-purple flowers which grow in smaller, less spreading clusters than those of the butterfly-weed. The swamp milkweed may be found in nearly all wet meadows. It is described by Gray as "rose-purple," but the finer specimens might almost claim to be ranked among the red flowers.

The dull pink balls of the common milkweed or silkweed are massed by every road-side now, and are too generally known to need description. The most delicate member of the family is the four-leaved milkweed, with fragrant pale pink blossoms which appear in June on the wooded hill-sides. Although there are eighteen distinct species of milkweed proper, perhaps the above are the only ones which are commonly encountered. Few plant-families add more to the beauty of the summer fields. But although its different representatives are deemed worthy of careful cultivation in other countries — the well-known swallow-worts of English gardens being milk-weeds —I doubt if the average American knows even the commoner species by sight, so careless have we been of our native flowers.

July yields no plant which is more perfect in both flower and foliage than the meadow-lily. It is a genuine delight to wade knee-deep into some meadow among the myriad erect stems, which are surrounded by symmetrical circles of lance-shaped leaves and crowned with long-stemmed, shaped leaves and crowned with long-stemmed, nodding, recurved lilies; lilies so bell-like and tremulous that such a meadow always suggests to me possibilities of tinkling music too ethereal for mortal ears. Usually these flowers are yellow, thickly spotted with brown, but this year I find them of the deepest shade of orange. Within the flower-cup the stamens are heavily loaded with brown pollen.

When with rhythmical sweep of his long scythe the mower lays low whole acres of lilies and clover, milkweeds, daisies, and buttercups, there is a tendency to bewail such a massacre of the flowers. But, after all, this is no purposeless destruction. As the dead blossoms lie heaped one upon another in the blazing sunlight, their sweetness is scattered abroad with every breath of wind. As we rest among the fragrant mounds we are still subject to their pervading influence. They "were lovely and pleasant in their lives, and in their death they were not divided."

But it is not the sentimentalist only who begrudges every flower that is picked without purpose, to be thrown aside, a repulsive, disfigured object, a few moments later. Certainly it seems unintelligent, if not wasteful and irreverent, to be possessed with an irresistible desire wantonly to destroy an exquisite organism. Yet so frequent is this form of unintelligence that, when the companioned flower-lover discovers a group of what he fears might be considered tempting blossoms, his instinct is to pounce upon them with outstretched arms and protect them from an almost certain onslaught.

Thoreau says somewhere that life should be lived "as tenderly and daintily as one would pluck a flower," so it is possible that in the neighborhood of Walden the ruthless flower-gatherers were in the minority, for one would regret to see a life lived as roughly and without semblance of daintiness as in less fortunate localities one can see flowers plucked by the dozen.

In the woods and along the thicket-bordered fields the vivid cups of the wood-lily gleam from clusters of dull bracken or from feathery, gold-tinged fern-beds. These had never seemed to me so almost blood-like in color as when I caught constant glimpses of them from the train a few days ago. As it had been raining heavily, I thought that the unusual intensity of their hue might be due to a recent bath. But in my wanderings since then I have encountered equally brilliant specimens, and again conclude that the flowers of this year are unusually deep-hued and vigorous.

However much we may revel in rich color, it is restful, after a time, to turn from these blazing children of the sun to the green water-courses which are marked by the white, pyramidal clusters and graceful foliage of the tall meadow-rue. On certain of these plants the flowers are exquisitely delicate and feathery, while on others they are comparatively coarse and dull. A closer inspection reveals that the former are the male, the latter the female flowers.

This distinction between the sexes, however, is less marked in the world of flowers than in that of birds. During the past week I have watched the comings and goings of a scarlet tanager, which had built his nest in the fork of a pine-tree within easy view of my window, and have had ample opportunity to contrast the tropical brilliancy of his plumage with the dull greenish dress of his mate, a contrast greater than any I have noticed among similarly related flowers.

Almost as refreshing as the masses of meadow-rue are the thickets composed of the deep green leaves and white, spreading flowers of the elder. Another beautiful shrub, which is now blossoming in marshy places, especially near the coast, is the fragrant white swamp honeysuckle. Only among the sand-hills of the coast itself do we meet with the purplish blossoms of the beach-pea. Nearly akin to it is the blue vetch, whose long, dense, one-sided clusters of small, pea-like flowers make little lakes of pinkish blue in wet meadows farther inland.

In the dry woods we encounter constantly a

shrubby plant with rounded clusters of small white flowers. This is the New Jersey tea, or red-root; the former name arising from the use made of its leaves during the Revolution, the latter from its dark red root. The driest and most uninviting localities do not seem to discourage either this persistent little shrub or the bushy-looking wild-indigo, with its clover-like leaves and short terminal clusters of yellow, pea-like blossoms.

In shaded hollows and on the hill-sides the tall white wands of the black cohosh, or bug-bane, shoot upward, rocket-like. The great stout stems, large divided leaves and slender spikes of feathery flowers render this the most conspicuous wood-plant of the season. If we chance to be lingering

"In secret paths that thread the forest land"

when the last sunlight has died away, and happen suddenly upon one of these ghostly groups, the effect is almost startling. The rank odor of the flowers detracts somewhat from one's enjoyment of their beauty, and is responsible, I suppose, for their unpleasing title of bugbane.

Under the pine-trees are the glossy leaves and nodding bells of the wintergreen; while here and there spring graceful, wax-like clusters of parasitic Indian pipe, the fresh blossoms nodding from leafless, fleshy stalks, the older ones erecting

PURPLE MILKWOOD
Asclepias purpurascens

themselves preparatory to fruiting. When we pick these odd-looking flowers they turn black from our touch, adding their protest to the cry against the despoiler, and invalidating their claim to the title which they sometimes bear of "corpse-plant."

From some deep shadow gleam the coral-like berries of the early elder or the bright, rigid clusters of the baneberry. On the low bush-honeysuckle the deep-colored yellow blossoms announce to the insect world that they have no attractions to offer in the way of pollen or honey, their fertilization being achieved already.

But at present the woods are not altogether satisfactory hunting-grounds. The more interesting flowers have sought the combined light and moisture of the open bogs or the sunshine of the fields and road-sides. Along the latter are quantities of bladder-campion, a European member of the pink family which has established itself in eastern New England. It can be recognized at once by its much-inflated calyx and by its deeply parted white petals. A few days since I found the wayside whitened with the large flowers of the lovely summer anemone, each one springing from between two closely set, deeply cut leaves, in the distance suggesting white wild-geraniums. A near kinsman, the thimble-weed, is apt to be confused with the summer anemone when it is found bearing white instead of greenish flowers. This curious-looking plant is noticeable now in shaded spots, growing to a height of two or three feet, and sending up gaunt flower-stalks which are finally crowned with a large, oblong, thimble-like head of fruit.

Banked in hollows of the hill-side are tall, nodding wands of willow-herb or fire-weed, with delicate flowers of intense purple-pink. Each blossom contains both stamens and pistil, but these mature at different times, and so-called "self-fertilization" is prevented. The pollen is discharged from the stamens while the immature pistil is still bent backward, with its stigmas so closed as to render it impossible for them to receive upon their surfaces a single quickening grain. Later it erects itself, spreading its four stigmas, which now secure easily any pollen which may have been brushed upon the body of the visiting bee. These flowers are so large and are visited so constantly by bees that anyone who chances upon the plant can witness speedily the whole performance.

Here are raspberry bushes covered thickly with fruit, so thickly that one could live for days on the rocky hill-side without other food than this most subtly flavored of all berries. Overhead its purple-flowered sister betrays its kinship with the now abundant wild-rose, whose delicate beauty it fails utterly to rival. In the low thicket are tiny, rose-veined bells of dogbane, and, beyond, the bright if somewhat ragged yellow flowers and dotted leaves of the irrepressible St. Johnswort jut up everywhere.

The umbrella-like clusters of the water-hemlock fill the moist ditches and suggest the wild-carrot of the later year; close by, the coarse stems and flat, yellow tops of its relative, the meadow parsnip, crowd one upon another. Farther on are soft plumes of the later yellow loosestrife, with little flowers similar to those of the four-leaved loosestrife, which is now on the wane.

One looks down upon a wood from whose edges gleam silvery birches, whose tops are soft with the tassels of the chestnut. Below it slopes a meadow turned yellow with the pale flowers of the wild-radish. Above it surges a field of grain which grows dark and cool with the shadow of a scurrying cloud. If one were nearer he would see among the wheat the bright pink-purple petals and green ruff-like calyx of the corn-cockle.

The year is at its height. The bosom of the earth is soft and restful as that of a mother. One abides in the perfect present, looking neither behind nor before. With the ever-recurring scent of new-mown hay comes another odor, aromatic, permeating. From our feet slopes

"— a bank where the wild thyme grows."

Only in this one spot have I ever met with this classic little plant, with its close purple flowers and tiny rigid leaves. When I first discovered it, one superb rain-washed afternoon, the line

"From dewy pastures, uplands sweet with
thyme,"

from Mr. Watson's poem on Wordsworth, flashed into my mind, and for the hundredth time I appreciated the rather flippant humor of someone's assertion that the chief use of Nature is to illustrate quotations from the poets.

 **9**

EARLY
AUGUST

It seems as if the day was not wholly profane
in which we have given heed to some natural
object.

— EMERSON

If someone should ask me to show him the place of all others which would reveal the largest number of striking flowers peculiar to this season, I should like to guide him to a certain salt-marsh — a salt-marsh which is cut up here and there by little inlets, where the water runs up at high tide and laps its way far inland, and which is dotted by occasional islands of higher, drier land that are covered with tall trees.

In the distance the marsh only looks refreshingly green, but if we draw nearer we see patches of vivid coloring for which the bright grass of the salt-meadows fails to account. If we enter it by way of the sand-hills on the beach, we almost hesitate to step upon the dainty carpet which lies before us. Hundreds of sea-pinks, or *Sabatia,* gleam like rosy stars above the grasses. Yet the prodigal fashion in which this plant lavishes its rich color upon the meadows does not constitute its sole or even its chief claim upon our enthusiasm, for it is as perfect in detail as it is beautiful in the mass. The five-parted corolla is of the purest pink, with clear markings of red and yellow at its centre. As in the willow-herb or fireweed, the stamens and pistils mature at different times, and self-fertilization is avoided.

One peculiarly large and beautiful species is *Sabatia chloroides*. This is found bordering brackish ponds along the coast. I have never been so fortunate as to see it growing, but specimens have been sent me from Cape Cod. A less conspicuous kind abounds in the rich soil of the interior.

Another abundant plant which is sure to excite our interest is the sea-lavender. Its small lavender-colored flowers are spiked along one side of the leafless, branching stems, giving a misty effect which makes its other common name of marsh rosemary seem peculiarly appropriate, when we know that the title is derived from the Latin for "sea-spray."

Here, too, we find the mock bishop-weed, one of the most delicate of the parsleys, with thread-like leaves and tiny white flowers growing in bracted clusters, the shape of which might suggest to the imaginative a bishop's cap. Through this veil of flower and foliage we spy the pinkish stems,

MOUNTAIN MAPLE
Acer spicatum

opposite, clasping leaves, and small flesh-colored blossoms of the marsh St. Johnswort, an attractive plant whose chief charm, perhaps, lies in its foliage and coloring, as its flowers, although pretty, are rather small and inconspicuous.

Parts of the meadow are bright with the oblong, clover-like heads of the milkwort. These seem to deepen in color from day to day till finally they look almost red. They are closely related to the lovely fringed polygala of the June woods, and to the little moss-like species with narrow leaves growing in circles about its stem, and thick flower-heads of purplish-pink, which can be found along the inner borders of this same marsh.

There is a hollow in the meadow which is always too wet to be explored comfortably without rubber-boots, and which becomes at high tide a salt-water pond. Its edges are guarded by ranks of tall swamp mallows, whose great rose-colored flowers flutter like banners in the breeze. Close by are thickets turned pinkish-purple by the dense flower-clusters of the largest and most showy of the tick-trefoils, a group of plants which are now in full bloom and which can be recognized by their three-divided leaves, pink or purple pea-like flowers, and by the flat, roughened pods which adhere to our clothes with regrettable pertinacity. The botany assigns this species to rich woods, but I have never seen it more abundant than here.

Only by pushing our way through a miniature forest composed of the purple-streaked stems, divided leaves, and white flowers of another parsley, the water-hemlock, do we reach the stretch of land which glories in the treasure which makes this especial marsh more brilliant and unusual than the many others which skirt the coast. This treasure is the yellow-fringed orchis, a plant which rears its full orange-colored domes on every side, making a mass of burning color in the morning sunlight.

I have never found an orchid growing in such abundance elsewhere, and cannot but hope that the meadow will guard its secret, lest some wholesale despoiler should contrive to rob it permanently of its greatest beauty. Certain orchids which were abundant formerly in parts of England can no longer be found in that country, owing to the reckless fashion in which the plants, for various purposes, were uprooted and carried off. It is well, too, to remember that plucking all of its flowers is equivalent to uprooting the plant in the case of annuals and biennials, as the future life of the species depends upon the seeds which the flowers set.

In the swamps farther inland the close white heads of the button-bush yield a jasmine-like fragrance. From grassy hummocks nod the violet-purple blossoms of the monkey-flower. The path

of the slow stream is defined by the bright arrow-
shaped leaves and spotless gold-centred flowers of
the arrow-head. About the upper part of their
stems are clustered the male blossoms, their three
snowy petals surrounding the yellow stamens, the
rather ugly female flowers with their dull green
centres occupying a less conspicuous position below. This is only in some cases, however; at times
the staminate and pistillate blossoms are found on
separate plants.

The edges of the pond are blue with the long,
close spikes of the pickerel-weed. Over the thickets on its shore the clematis has flung a veil of
feathery white. A tangle of golden threads with
little bunched white flowers shows that the dodder
is at its old game of living on its more self-reliant
neighbors. From erect, finger-like clusters comes
the sweet, spicy breath of the *Clethra*.

Where the white dust of the road powders the
wayside plants, rise the coarse stalks of the evening primrose. These are hung with faded-look-
ing flowers whose unsuspectedly fragrant petals
gleamed through the moonlit darkness of last
night. Among them we find a fragile, canary-
yellow blossom which has been unable to close
because the pink night-moth, which is the plant's
regular visitor, is so overcome with sleep, or so
drunk, perhaps, with nectar, that it is quite obliv-
ious of the growing day and of its host's custom

of closing its doors with sunrise. We are so un-used to seeing these gay creatures that we feel a little as if we had surprised some ballroom beauty fast asleep on the scene of her midnight triumphs.

The slender spikes of the tall purple vervain have a somewhat jagged appearance, owing to the reluctance of its little deep-hued flowers to open simultaneously. The mullein is not without this same peculiarity. Its sleepy-looking blossoms open one by one, giving the dense spike an unfin-ished, sluggish aspect. In fact, I think it is the most "logy" looking plant we have. Although it came to us originally from England, it is now comparatively rare in that country. Mr. Bur-roughs quotes a London correspondent, who says that when one comes up in solitary glory its ap-pearance is heralded much as if it were a comet, the development of its woolly leaves and the growth of its spike being watched and reported upon day by day.

The broad, butterfly-shaped flowers of the moth-mullein, another emigrant, are much more pleasing than those of its kinsman. Its corolla is sometimes white, sometimes yellow, with a dash of red or purple at the centre. Its stamens are loaded with orange-colored pollen and bearded with tufts of violet wool, which we fancy shields some hidden nectar, as its whole appearance sug-gests that it aims to attract insect visitors.

Despite the aversion with which it is regarded by the farmers, and the carelessness with which it is overlooked by those who value only the unusual, the wild-carrot is one of the most beautiful of our naturalized plants. There is a delicacy and symmetry in the feathery clusters suggestive of cobwebs, of magnified snowflakes, of the finest of laces (one of its common names is Queen Anne's lace), of the daintiest creations in the worlds of both art and nature.

Perhaps the most omnipresent flower just now is the yarrow. Its finely dissected leaves and close white clusters border every road-side. Indeed, when passing through New York a short time ago it showed its familiar face in a Fifth Avenue dooryard. Despite what seems to me an obvious unlikeness, it is confused frequently with the wild-carrot. Five minutes' study of the two plants with a common magnifying-glass will fix firmly in the mind the difference between them. It requires little botanical knowledge to recognize at once that the wild-carrot is a member of the umbelliferous parsley family. But the small heads of the yarrow so perfectly simulate separate flowers that this plant is less readily identified as a composite.

Huddled in hollows by the road-side are the tall stout stalks, clasping woolly leaves, and great yellow disks of the elecampane, another composite. Still another, which is never found far from the highway, is the chicory, the charm of whose sky-blue flowers is somewhat decreased by the bedraggled appearance of the rest of the plant.

Every true-born American ought to recognize the opposite, widely spreading leaves, and dull, whitish flower-clusters of the boneset, a plant which cured, or which was supposed to cure, so many of the ailments of our forefathers. Even to-day the country children eye it ruefully as it hangs in long dried bunches in the attic, waiting to be brewed at the slightest warning into a singularly nauseating draught.

Nearly related to the boneset proper is the Joe-Pye-weed, with tall stout stems surrounded by circles of rough oblong leaves, and with intensely purple-pink flowers, which are massing themselves effectively in the low meadows. In parts of the country no plant does more for the beauty of the landscape of late summer. It is said to have taken its name from an Indian medicine-man, who found it a cure for typhus fever.

The European bellflower has become naturalized in New England, and the road-sides now are bright with its graceful lilac-blue spires. Another brilliant immigrant which is blossoming at present is the purple loosestrife. The botany extends its range from Nova Scotia to Delaware, but I find its myriad deep-hued wands only on the swampy shores of the Hudson, and in the marshes which have for their background the level outline of the Shawangunk Mountains.

Along shaded streams the jewel-weeds hang their spurred, delicate pockets; these are sometimes pale yellow, again deep orange, spotted with reddish-brown. In certain swampy woods and open marshes we discover the feathery pink-purple spikes of the smaller fringed orchis.

Summer seems well advanced when the curved leafy stems of the Solomon's seal and twisted-stalk are hung, the first with blackish, the second with bright red berries. Except in the open fields, fruits now are more conspicuous than flowers. Of the latter, in the woods, we note chiefly the pink blossoms strung upon the long leafless stalks of the tick-trefoil, also a somewhat similar-looking plant, the lop-seed, whose small pink flowers are not pea-like, however, and whose leaves are not divided, as are those of the trefoils. The inconspicuous, two-petalled blossoms and thin opposite leaves of the uninteresting enchanter's nightshade are abundant everywhere.

On the hill-side the velvety crimson plumes of the staghorn sumach toss upward in the pride of fruition. Here the soft cushion of the pasture-thistle yields a pleasant fragrance, and violet patches are made in the grass by the incomplete heads of the self-heal. Against the dark oval leaves of the cockspur-thorn lie red-cheeked, apple-like fruit. Currant-like clusters of choke-cherries hang from the thicket. The birds are twittering with joy at the feast which the black-cap bushes are yielding, and a song-sparrow flies to the top of a red-osier dogwood, which is heavy with its burden of white berries, and gives vent to a few bubbling notes with an ecstatic energy which threatens almost to burst its little body.

～ 10 ～

GOLDEN-ROD
AND ASTER

Along the road-side, like the flowers of gold
That tawny Incas for their gardens wrought,
Heavy with sunshine droops the golden-rod,
And the red pennons of the cardinal-flower
Hang motionless upon their upright staves.

— WHITTIER

IN AN INTERESTING ARTICLE on "American Wild-Flowers" which appeared in *The Fortnightly Review* some years ago, the English naturalist, Mr. Alfred Wallace, commented upon the fact, or what seemed to him the fact, that nowhere in our country could be seen any such brilliant masses of flowers as are yearly displayed by the moors and meadows of Great Britain.

I have not the article with me and do not recall certainly whether Mr. Wallace saw our fields and hill-sides in their September dress, but I do remember that he dwelt chiefly upon our earlier flowers, and while, of course, he alluded to the many species of golden-rods and asters to be found in the United States, it seems to me quite impossible that he could have seen our country at this season and yet have remained unconvinced of the unusual brilliancy of its flora.

Despite the beauty of our woods and meadows when starred with the white of bloodroot and anemone, and with the purple-red of the wake-robin, they are perhaps less radiant than those of England "in primrose-time." And although our summer landscape glows with deep-hued lilies and milkweeds, and glitters with black-eyed Susans, yet in actual brilliancy it must yield the palm to an English field of scarlet poppies. But when September lines the road-sides of New England with the purple of the aster, and flings its mantle of golden-rod over her hills, and fills her hollows with the pink drifts of the Joe-Pye-weed or with the intense red-purple of the iron-weed, and guards her brooks with tall ranks of yellow sunflowers, then I think that any moor or meadow of Great Britain might be set in her midst and yet fail to pale her glory.

Of the hundred or so classified species of golden-rod, about eighty belong to the United States. Of these some forty can be found in our Northeastern States. The scientific name of the genus, *Solidago,* signifying "to make whole," refers to the faith which formerly prevailed in its healing powers. It belongs to the composite family, which now predominates so generally. Its small heads are composed of both ray and disk flowers, which are of the same golden hue, except in one species. These flower-heads are usually clustered in one-sided racemes, which spring from the upper part of a leafy stem.

One of the commonest species, and one of the earliest to blossom, is the rough golden-rod, a plant with hairy stem, thick, rough, oblong leaves, and small heads, each one of which is made up of from seven to nine ray-flowers and from four to seven disk-flowers. Occasionally it will be found growing to a height of five or six feet, but ordinarily it is one of the lowest of the genus. The elm-leaved species is a somewhat similar-looking plant, with thinner, larger leaves, a smooth stem, and with only about four ray-flowers to each little head. The so-called Canadian golden-rod, with its tall, stout stem, pointed, sharply toothed leaves and short ray-flowers, is one of the commonest varieties.

The lance-leaved species is seldom recognized as a member of the tribe, because of its flat-topped clusters, which form a striking contrast to the slender, wand-like racemes which usually characterize the genus. It is often mistaken for the tansy, which is also a yellow composite, but which is quite dissimilar in detail, having deeply divided leaves, the segments of which are cut and toothed, and sometimes much crisped and curled, and button-like, deep-hued flower-heads, which appear to be devoid of ray-flowers. Strictly speaking, the tansy is not a wild flower with us. It was brought from Europe to the gardens of New England, where it was raised as a valuable weed. Now it dyes yellow the hollows of the abandoned homestead and strays lawlessly to the borders of the highway.

The tribe of asters is even larger than that of golden-rods, numbering some two hundred species. Italy, Switzerland, and Great Britain each yield but one native variety, I believe, although others are largely cultivated, the Christmas and Michaelmas daisies of English gardens being American asters. One species, *Aster glacialis* of the botanies, is found growing 12,000 feet above the sea. The blue and purple varieties, those having blue and purple ray-flowers, that is, are much commoner than those with white ray-flowers. Over fifty of the former are found in the Northeastern States to about a dozen of the latter.

Of the white species, the earliest to blossom is the corymbed aster, which can be identified by its slender, somewhat zigzag stems, its thin, heart-shaped leaves, and its loosely clustered flower-heads. It grows plentifully in the open woods, especially somewhat northward. In swamps and moist thickets we find the umbelled aster, with its long, tapering leaves, and flat clusters, which it lifts at times to a height of seven feet. A beautiful variety which is abundant along the coast is the many-flowered aster. This is a bushy, spreading plant, somewhat suggestive of an evergreen, with little, narrow, rigid leaves, and small, crowded flower-heads.

The tall, stout stems and large violet heads of the New England aster mark one of the most striking of the purple species. It floods with color the low meadows and moist hollows along the road-side, while the wood-borders are lightened by the pale blue rays of the heart-leaved variety.

There are many other species without English titles which can hardly be described without the aid of technical terms. Even the trained botanist finds himself daunted at times in his efforts to identify the various species, while the beginner is sure to be sorely tried if he sets himself this task. Yet if he perseveres he will be rewarded, as every road-side will supply an absorbing problem; for there is a decided fascination in detecting the individual traits of plants that to the untrained eye have nothing to distinguish them from one another. The significance of the scientific title of the genus *Aster* is easily appreciated, for the effect of its flowers is peculiarly star-like.

The red-purple clusters of the iron-weed are often mistaken for asters by those who are not sufficiently observant to notice that its flower-heads are composed entirely of tubular blossoms, being without the ray-flowers which are essential to an aster. In the iron-weed the involucre of little leaf-like scales which always surrounds the flower-head of a composite, and which is commonly considered a calyx by the unbotanical, is usually of a purplish tint, each little scale being tipped with a tiny cusp or point. Its alternate leaves are long and narrow, and its tough stem is responsible for its common name. Its scientific title, *Vernonia,* was bestowed in honor of an English botanist who travelled in this country many years ago.

In the rich woods the flat-topped flower-clusters and broad, pointed leaves of the white snake-root, a near relative of the boneset, are noticeable. This is a brighter-looking, more ornamental plant than its celebrated kinsman. Along the streams and in the thickets the sunflowers lift their yellow heads far above our own, while the wet ditches are gilded with the bright rays of the bur-marigold.

Somewhat southward the large heads of the so-called golden aster (which is not an aster at all) star the dry fields and road-sides. In moist, shaded spots we find the ephemeral day-flower, or *Commelina,* with its two sky-blue petals quaintly commemorating the two Commelyns (distinguished Dutch botanists), while the odd petal, which can boast little in the way of either size or color, immortalizes the comparative insignificance of a less renowned brother. At least so runs the tradition.

NEW ENGLAND ASTER
Aster novae-angliae

From barren sandy banks in much the same latitudes spring the branching stems, opposite aromatic leaves, and clustered, delicate white or lavender-colored flowers of the dittany, one of the mints. On the hill-side the little corollas of the blue-curls are falling so as to reveal within the calyx the four tiny nutlets, which are a prominent characteristic of the same family, while the plant's clammy, balsam-scented leaves offer another means of identification.

Near the blue-curls we are likely to find the closely spiked, pea-like blossoms and three-divided leaves of the bush-clover, as well as the pink-purple flowers and downy and also clover-like foliage of another of the tick-trefoils. As these two groups of plants have so many points in common that it is somewhat difficult ordinarily to distinguish between them, it is well to remember that the calyx of a tick-trefoil is usually more or less two-lipped, while that of a bush-clover is divided into five slender and nearly equal lobes.

Two other members of the pulse or pea family are frequently encountered during the earliest part of this month. Along the grassy lanes that wind in and out among the woods are delicate clusters of pale lilac blossoms nodding from a stem which clambers over the thicket and twines about the iron-weeds and asters. I believe this graceful plant owes its unattractive name of hog-peanut to its underground fruit, which is said to be uprooted and devoured by hogs. In low places, climbing about whatever shrub or plant it chances to find, grows the wild-bean, with thick clusters of brown and pinkish flowers which yield a delicate fragrance somewhat suggestive of violets. My experience has been that these four members of the pulse family are especially abundant along the coast.

The salt-meadows are bright with the purplish-pink shells of the sea-side gerardia. These flowers, although smaller, are almost identical in shape with those of their relative, the yellow false foxglove, which we found in the woods some time ago. The slender gerardia is a similar-looking plant which abounds farther inland. This genus is named after the early botanist, Gerarde, author of the famous "Herball." Its members are supposed to be more or less parasitic in their habits, drawing their nourishment from the roots of other plants. For some time the pale foliage of the salt-marsh fleabane has been conspicuous by contrast among the daily deepening flower-heads of the milkwort and the bright green leaves of the marsh St. Johnswort, and finally it spreads before us its pink clusters of tiny, strongly scented flowers.

Some weeks since I described the pickerel-weed and arrow-head as in their prime, but it must be remembered that a plant which flowers in

August in southern New York and New Jersey may not blossom in the mountains farther north until September. Along the Saranac River in the Adirondacks a few days ago I found the pickerel-weed more fully and luxuriantly in bloom than on any previous occasion. The slender spikes of delicate blue flowers reared themselves above great beds of dark, polished leaves, making a rich border to the winding river. Our guide told us that in spring the pickerel laid their eggs among these plants, which at that season are not visible above the water, and that later the moose fed upon their leaves.

The shoals were still starred with the pure blossoms of the arrow-head, while in the current of the stream trembled the thick pink spikes of the amphibious knot-weed. At the foot of the rush-like leaves and golden-brown spires of the cat-tail, and among the soft round heads of the bur-reed, protruded the knobby buds and coarse, bright flowers of the yellow pond-lily. In places where the logs sent down the river the previous winters had "jammed," the fuzzy, whitish pyramids of the meadow-sweet spired upward by the hundred.

On the banks the blossoms of the fire-weed had made way for the pink, slender pods which were about to crack open, releasing cloudy masses of silver-winged seeds. Great clusters of delicate

Osmunda ferns leaned over the water's edge. The tall stems and white, huddled flowers of the turtle-head hardly succeeded in keeping out of the stream. As a dark curve of shore swept in sight, against its background of spruce, birch, hemlock, and balsam-fir gleamed

> "The cardinal and the blood-red spots,
> Its double in the stream."

In this flower seems to culminate the vivid beauty of the summer. Yet, despite its intense color, it is so sure to choose a cool, rich setting that it never suggests heat, as do the field flowers of the earlier year.

Many of the lily-pads had been turned over by the swift current, or, perhaps, by a passing boat, and showed the deep, polished pink of their lower sides. Thick among them floated their placid, queenly flowers, with their green and pink-tinged sepals, and their snowy petals which pass imperceptibly into the centre of golden stamens. The bright red twigs of the dog-wood, the coral clusters of the now beautiful hobble-bush, and a stray branch of crimson maple lightened the more thickly wooded banks.

As we left the boat, stepping upon the elastic carpet of moss and pine-needles, and crossing a fallen, lichen-grown tree-trunk, we discovered the low white flowers and violet-like leaves of the

Dalibarda, and were filled with wonder and delight when we found the pink, fragrant bells of the *Linnaea* still heralding the fame of their great master. The tiny, evergreen, birch-flavored leaves of the creeping snowberry almost hid from view its spotless fruit, but the peculiarly bright-blue berries of the *Clintonia* were everywhere conspicuous as they rose above their large polished leaves. Among delicate masses of the clover-like foliage of the wood-sorrel lurked a late pink-veined blossom. And where we looked only for gleaming clusters of scarlet fruit we found the white, petal-like leaves of the bunchberry. If in June we were saddened by the first transmutations of flower into fruit, apparent symbols of a year that is no longer young, in September we are compensated by these unexpected emblems of its eternal youth.

❧ 11 ❧

AUTUMN

Oh, sacrament of summer days,
Oh, last communion in the haze,
Permit a child to join,

Thy sacred emblems to partake,
Thy consecrated bread to break,
Taste thine immortal wine!

— EMILY DICKINSON

On every perfect day, Nature, like a beautiful woman, cajoles her true lovers into the belief that she has never before worn so becoming a dress. I have a conviction of long standing that the world is fairest when the trees are first laced with green, and little tender things are pushing up everywhere and bursting into miracles of delicate bloom. Yet, with each heaven-born morning of the succeeding seasons, this somewhat spasmodic faith is weakly surrendered. It is impossible to wonder at Lowell's

"What is so rare as a day in June?"

when the lanes are first lined with white-flowered shrubs, and the air is heavy with fragrance and alive with bird-voices. Later, without one backward glance, I abandon myself to the ripe, luscious beauty of midsummer. And though, while taking my first fall walk the other day (for the true fall is not here till well on in September), and while noting how the hills were veiled by a silvery mist, and how the road-sides wore a many-hued embroidery, and that the sumach in the swamp was beginning to look like the burning bush on Horeb, I felt that there could be no beauty like this, which foretold the end; yet already I realize that before long the purple shadows will lie so softly upon the snowy fields, and the faint rose of dawn or twilight will flush with such tenderness the white side of the mountain, that the earth may seem lovelier in her shroud than in any of her living garments.

But it is altogether human to set especial value upon the things of which we are about to be deprived, and now, more than ever, we linger out of doors, yielding ourselves to influences which lie upon our spirits like a benediction, storing our minds with images which, among less inspiring surroundings, will

> "flash upon that inward eye,
>   Which is the bliss of
>   solitude."

Few flowers are abroad, barring the asters and golden-rods, yet these few we invest with a peculiar interest and affection, experiencing a sensation of gratitude, almost, as toward some beings who have stood stanch when the multitudes fell away.

No group of plants belong more distinctively to the season than do the gentians. Of these, the most famous, though by no means the most frequent representative is the fringed gentian, a flower which owes, I fancy, much of its reputation to Bryant's well-known lines; not that it does not deserve the interest which has centred about it, but that, while everyone has heard of it, comparatively few people seem to have ferreted out its haunts. Probably Bryant, also, is largely responsible for the somewhat inaccurate notions which are afloat concerning its usual season of blooming. This is in September, long before the

"woods are bare and birds are flown";

although Thoreau, if I remember rightly, records that he found it in flower as late as November 7th, when, certainly,

"frosts and shortening days portend
The aged year is near his end."

My first fringed gentian was the reward of a forty-mile drive, taken one cold autumn day for the sole purpose of paying court to its blue loveliness. It enticed us into a wet, green meadow where, picking our way from hummock to hummock, without appreciably diminishing the supply, we gathered one tall cluster after another of the delicate, deep-hued blossoms. In bud the fringed petals are twisted one about the other. When the day is cloudy, or even, I should judge, if the wind is high, the full-blown flower closes in the same fashion. The individuals which grow in the shade are even more attractive than those which frequent the open. Their blue is lighter, with a silvery tinge which I do not recall in any other flower. Until this year I have never encountered the plant in my ordinary wanderings, but during the past few days I have found it bordering in abundance the Berkshire lanes. Being an annual, we cannot predict with certainty its whereabouts from year to year, as its seeds may be washed to some distance in the moist regions which usually it favors.

Far less delicate and uncommon, but still attractive, is the closed gentian. This is usually a stout, rather tall plant, with crowded clusters of deep blue or purple flowers, which never open, looking always like buds. It grows along the shaded road-sides, and is easily confused with other members of the group, as both the five-flowered and soapwort gentians have narrow corollas, which often appear almost closed.

Certain New England woods and road-sides are now tinged with the pale blue or at times pinkish blossoms of the five-flowered species, while in the Adirondacks in early September, parts of the shore of the Raquette River were actually "blued" with what I take to have been the lance-leaved gentian, *Gentiana linearis* of the botany, formerly considered a variety of the soapwort species. This conjecture as to their identity was never verified, as the specimens gathered for analysis were thrown away by the guide during a storm which overtook us on one of the "carries."

In the wet meadows which harbor the fringed gentian we find also the white or cream-colored flowers of the grass of Parnassus, their five veiny petals crowning a tall, slender stem, which is clasped below by a little rounded leaf. There is a suggestion of spring in a fresh cluster of these blossoms, perhaps owing to a superficial resemblance to the anemones, or it may be because they have little of the hardy look of other fall flowers.

Here, too, abounds the last orchid of the year, the ladies' tresses, with small white flowers growing in a slender, twisted spike. Occasionally this plant becomes ambitious. Leaving the low, "wet places" to which it is assigned by the botany, it climbs far up the hill-sides. I never remember seeing it in greater abundance or more fragrant and perfect than in a field high up on the Catskill Mountains. The flowers that we care for we are

apt to associate with the particular spot in which
we found them first — or at their best — and the
mention or sight of this little orchid instantly recalls that breezy upland with its far-reaching view,
and its hum of eager bees, which were sucking
the rare sweets of the late year from the myriad
spires among which I lay one September morning.

Another plant linked for me with the same region and season is the so-called Canadian violet.
Till late September, along a winding mountain-
road, one could gather great bunches of its fresh,
leafy-stemmed flowers — white, yellow-centred,
fragrant, with purple veins above and violet-
washed below. Near them the wild-strawberries
were abundantly in blossom, as they are now to
some extent in Berkshire.

And whenever I see a depauperate mountain-
ash forlornly decorating a corner of some over-
civilized country-place, languishing like a handsome young barbarian in captivity, I remember
how that same road brought one to the forest
which crowned the mountain's top — to a dimly
lighted path, which led through mossy fern-beds
till it reached a sudden opening, where two great
hemlocks made a frame, and a dark, distant
mountain formed a background for the feathery
foliage and scarlet clusters of a superbly vigorous
specimen of this beautiful tree.

If we leave the mountains and visit once more

the salt-meadows, we notice a multitude of erect, narrow-leaved stems, which toward their summits are studded with soft, rose-purple flower-heads. This is the blazing star, one of the latest blooming and most beautiful of the composites.

Just back of the beach the gray sand-hills are warm with the slender branches and little rose-colored flowers of the sand knotweed, a patch of which reminded Thoreau of "a peach-orchard in bloom." The bright-hued, leafless stems of the glasswort define the borders of the road. Only a close examination convinces us of the existence of the minute flowers of this odd-looking plant, for they are so sunken in its thickened upper joints as to be almost invisible.

Now and then we come across an evening primrose with blossoms so wide open, delicate, and fragrant, and with leaf and stem so lacking their usual rankness, that we can hardly connect it with the great, coarse plants whose brown, flowerless spikes are crowding the edge of the highway. In this neighborhood the brilliant flowers and fleshy leaves of the sea-side golden-rod are everywhere conspicuous, while farther inland the so-called blue-stemmed species, bearing its clustered heads in the leaf-angles along the stem, begins to predominate. On the mountains and in the dry thickets of the lowlands we encounter occasionally one of the most attractive of the tribe — the sweet golden-rod, with shining, dotted, narrow leaves, which yield, when crushed, a refreshing, anise-like odor.

The different asters are affording the loveliest shades of blue, purple, and lavender. Pre-eminent for richness of color and beauty of detail are the large, violet-hued, daisy-like heads of the showy aster, a species which is found growing in sandy soil along the coast. In the woods, nodding from tall stems, we notice the graceful, bell-like flower-heads of the rattlesnake-root.

A friend writes me that in parts of Connecticut the swamps are still bright with the great blue lobelia, and that the yellow flowers of the bur-marigold are abundant in the road-side ditches. This last-named plant holds its own through the first frosts till well on in November. Its dull-looking sister, the common stick-tight, whose ugly, brownish flower-heads are frequent in moist, waste places, is equally tenacious of life — and of our clothes, to which its barbed seed-vessels cling so persistently that every walk across country means that we have innocently extended its un-welcome sway.

Indeed, we can hardly spend a morning out of doors at this season without having our attention drawn constantly to the many ingenious devices adopted by the different plants for the distribution of their seed. On ourselves and on our dogs we

HOBBLEBUSH
Viburnum alnifolium

find not only the troublesome barbs of the stick-tight, but also the flat, hooked pods of the tick-trefoils, the bristly fruit of avens and goose-grass, and the prickly heads of the burdock. In the thicket the birds are already stripping the dogwoods of their red, blue, and lead-colored berries, either releasing the seeds upon the spot or carrying them to some other and, perhaps, more hospitable neighborhood; while the coral beads of the beautiful black alder, the red or purple sprays of the viburnums, the bright haws of the white-thorn, the scarlet pennants which stream from the barberry bushes, and the half-hidden berries of the partridge-vine, tempt them to a feast which will prove as advantageous to host as to guest.

If the seeds are not trapped out in a fashion which renders them attractive to animals their transportation generally is provided in some other manner. Notice how the great pasture-thistle is slowly swelling into a silvery cushion which a few brisk winds will disintegrate. Watch the pods of the milkweed crack open, revealing symmetrical packs (the beloved "fishes" of childhood) of golden-brown seeds, to each one of which is tacked a silky sail which finally unfurls and floats away with its burden. Go down to the brook and finger lightly the pod of the jewel-weed, or touch-me-not. You will become so fascinated with the ingenious mechanism which causes the little seed-vessel to recoil from your touch with an elastic spring which sends the seeds far into the neighboring thicket, that you will hardly leave till the last tiny adventurer has been started on his life-journey.

On the hill-side grows a shrub with wavy-toothed leaves, and a nut-like fruit which has been ripening all summer. We know that this is the witch-hazel, because little bunches of fragrant, narrow-petalled yellow flowers are bursting from the branches. All the blossoms may not appear for some time yet, but when the fruit has ripened and the leaves are fallen they will surprise us like a golden prophecy of spring. Break off and carry home a fruiting branch. Soon the capsules will snap elastically apart, discharging in every direction their black, bony contents; the action of the parent plant somewhat recalling that of the mother bird who pushes her young from the edge of the nest that they may learn to shift for themselves.

Many seeds are washed by water to more or less remote neighborhoods. Some become attached with clods of earth to the feet of birds, and are borne to other regions, where they thrive or perish, according to their power of adapting themselves to their new environment. How far this last class of travellers may journey we realize especially at this season, when nearly every day shows us fresh flocks of birds which have come under the influence of that strange power which moves them "to stretch their wings toward the South," bringing them (even the more timid species) this morning to our very doorstep in search of food, inducing them to-night to resume a voyage which may terminate only in the tropics.

Each walk abroad brings up new questions for settlement. The last is one of preference pure and simple, namely, whether the "snake" fence or the stone wall affords the greater possibilities. Till recently I had no doubt as to the aesthetic superiority of the stone wall. It has such infinite capacity for tumbling, for taking on a coat of lichens and mosses — for wearing soft tints of time and weather. When quite prostrate, its ruin is hidden so tenderly by blood-red tangles of Virginia creeper or silky plumes of clematis, and by masses of soft ferns, which nestle lovingly about its feet. In the presence of the ideal stone wall — and I know a hundred such — there seems no room for indecision.

Yet the crooked course of the snake fence is undeniably picturesque. Its "zigzags" offer singularly choice retreats for great clumps of purple-stalked, red-stained, heavy-fruited poke-weed, for groups of yellow-brown *Osmunda* ferns, and for festoons of bitter-sweet, with orange pods split open to reveal their scarlet-coated seeds. No stone wall can yield such occasional vistas of

meadow beyond, bright with golden-rod and aster, and framed by brilliant strands of blackberry
vine. When its plants and shrubs and creepers are
left quite unmolested, free to follow its devious
course, to twine about its posts, or to peep con-
fidingly over its topmost rails, then, I own, my
loyalty begins to waver.

But after a time the rambler out of doors grows
accustomed to leaving his questions unanswered.
Plant-nature, especially, he finds almost as incon-
sistent and contradictory as his own. Surprises
soon cease to be surprising. Even now the rank
stems of the chicory are studded with bright blue
blossoms. The sun shines warm and sweet upon
grass which is green and tender as in June. Soothing insect-murmurs so fill the air that the absence
of bird-notes is hardly felt. Clover-heads are full
and deep-hued, yielding stores of nectar to the
bees. All about are bright groups of black-eyed
Susan — a plant which two months ago looked
brown and "done for." Feathery clusters of wild-
carrot spread themselves beside the fruiting um-
bels, which look like collapsed birds'-nests. Daisies are fresh, and buttercups so glossy that one
can hardly resist brushing them with one's lips to
see if they are actually wet.

Yet the maple which leans clear across the
brook is already crimson, and when we reach the
rocky hill-side the yellow fronds of the *Dicksonia*

exhale a subtle fragrance which suggests decay. Another faint, elusive odor, starting a train of equally elusive memories, floats upward from the only flower at our feet, the "life-everlasting," which, as children, I hardly know why, we always associated with graves. Here, where there is none of the life and freshness of the meadow below, it seems to decorate the grave of summer. Dr. Holmes says concerning it: "A something it has of sepulchral spicery, as if it had been brought from the core of some great pyramid, where it had lain on the breast of a mummied Pharaoh. Something, too, of immortality in the sad, faint sweetness lingering long in its lifeless petals. Yet this does not tell why it fills my eyes with tears, and carries me in blissful thought to the banks of asphodel that border the 'River of Life.'"